Microsoft® Office Word 2003

Level 1

Chris Blocher

Microsoft® Office Word 2003: Level 1

Part Number: 084360
Course Edition: 1.02

ACKNOWLEDGMENTS

Project Team

Senior Content Developer: Chris Blocher • **Content Manager:** Cheryl Russo • **Content Editors:** J-P Altieri, Peter Bauer, Christy Johnson and Laura Thomas • **Material Editors:** Elizabeth M. Swank and Frank Wosnick • **Graphic Designer:** Tracie Cole • **Project Technical Support:** Michael Toscano

NOTICES

HELP US IMPROVE OUR COURSEWARE

Your comments are important to us. Please contact us at Element K Press LLC, 1-800-478-7788, 500 Canal View Boulevard, Rochester, NY 14623, Attention: Product Planning, or through our Web site at **http://support.elementkcourseware.com.**

This logo means that this courseware has been approved by the Microsoft® Office Specialist Program to be among the finest available for learning Microsoft Word 2003. It also means that upon completion of this courseware, you may be prepared to take an exam for Microsoft Offices Specialist qualification.

What is a Microsoft Office Specialist? A Microsoft Office Specialist is an individual who has passed exams for certifying his or her skills in one or more of the Microsoft Office desktop applications such as Microsoft Word, Microsoft Excel, Microsoft PowerPoint, Microsoft Outlook, Microsoft Access, or Microsoft Project. The Microsoft Office Specialist Program typically offers certification exams at the "Core" and "Expert" skill levels. The Microsoft Office Specialist Program is the only program in the world approved by Microsoft for testing proficiency in Microsoft Office desktop applications and Microsoft Project. This testing program can be a valuable asset in any job search or career advancement.

To learn more about becoming a Microsoft Office Specialist, visit **www.microsoft.com/officespecialist**. To learn more about other Microsoft Office Specialist approved courseware from Element K, visit **www.elementkcourseware.com**.

*The availability of Microsoft Office Specialist certification exams varies by application, application version, and language. Visit **www.microsoft.com/officespecialist** for exam availability.

Element K is independent from Microsoft Corporation, and not affiliated with Microsoft in any manner. This publication may be used in assisting students to prepare for a Microsoft Office Specialist exam. Neither Microsoft, its designated program administrator or courseware reviewer, nor Element K warrants that use of this publication will ensure passing the relevant exam.

NOTES

MICROSOFT® OFFICE WORD 2003: LEVEL 1

LESSON 1: CREATING A BASIC DOCUMENT

LESSON 2: EDITING A DOCUMENT

Contents

Lesson 5: Proofing a Document

Lesson 6: Adding Tables

Lesson 7: Inserting Graphic Elements

ABOUT THIS COURSE

Word processing is the use of computers to create, revise, and save documents for printing and future retrieval. This course is the first in a series of three Microsoft® Office Word 2003 courses. It will provide you with the basic concepts required to produce basic business documents.

Historically, documents were painstakingly created and edited by hand. Over time, producing documents has become more efficient. Microsoft® Word 2003 makes creating and editing documents even easier by providing a user-friendly environment, enabling you to add text, graphics, tables, formatting, and more with just a few mouse clicks.

Course Description

Target Student

Persons with a basic understanding of Microsoft Windows who need to learn how to use Microsoft® Word 2003 to create, edit, format, lay out, and print standard business documents complete with tables and graphics. This course is intended for persons interested in pursuing Microsoft Office Specialist certification in Microsoft® Word 2003.

Course Prerequisites

This course assumes that you are familiar with using personal computers and have used a mouse and keyboard (basic typing skills are recommended). You should be comfortable in the Windows environment and be able to use Windows to manage information on your computer. Specifically, you should be able to launch and close programs; navigate to information stored on the computer; and manage files and folders. One of the following courses or equivalent knowledge is required:

- *Windows XP Professional: Level 1*
- *Windows XP Professional: Level 2*
- *Windows XP: Introduction*
- *Windows 2000: Introduction*

How to Use This Book

As a Learning Guide

Each lesson covers one broad topic or set of related topics. Lessons are arranged in order of increasing proficiency with *Microsoft® Word 2003*; skills you acquire in one lesson are used and developed in subsequent lessons. For this reason, you should work through the lessons in sequence.

We organized each lesson into results-oriented topics. Topics include all the relevant and supporting information you need to master *Microsoft® Word 2003*, and activities allow you to apply this information to practical hands-on examples.

You get to try out each new skill on a specially prepared sample file. This saves you typing time and allows you to concentrate on the skill at hand. Through the use of sample files, hands-on activities, illustrations that give you feedback at crucial steps, and supporting background information, this book provides you with the foundation and structure to learn *Microsoft® Word 2003* quickly and easily.

As a Review Tool

Any method of instruction is only as effective as the time and effort you are willing to invest in it. In addition, some of the information that you learn in class may not be important to you immediately, but it may become important later on. For this reason, we encourage you to spend some time reviewing the topics and activities after the course. For additional challenge when reviewing activities, try the "What You Do" column before looking at the "How You Do It" column.

As a Reference

The organization and layout of the book make it easy to use as a learning tool and as an after-class reference. You can use this book as a first source for definitions of terms, background information on given topics, and summaries of procedures.

Microsoft Word 2003: Level 1 is one of a series of Element K courseware titles that addresses Microsoft Office Specialist skill sets. The Office Specialist program is for individuals who use Microsoft's business desktop software and who seek recognition for their expertise with specific Microsoft products. Certification candidates must pass one or more product proficiency exams in order to earn Office Specialist certification.

Course Objectives

In this course, you will create, edit, and enhance standard business documents using Microsoft® Office Word 2003.

You will:

- create a basic document.
- edit documents by locating and modifying text.
- format text.
- format paragraphs.

- use Word tools to make your documents more accurate.
- add tables to a document.
- add graphic elements to a document.
- control a document's page setup and its overall appearance.

Course Requirements

Hardware

For this course, you will need one computer for each student and one for the instructor. Each computer will need the following minimum hardware components:

- A 233 MHz Pentium-class processor if you use Windows XP Professional as your operating system. 300 MHz is recommended.
- A 133 MHz Pentium-class processor if you use Windows 2000 Professional as your operating system.
- 128 MB of RAM.
- A 6 GB hard disk or larger.
- A floppy disk drive.
- A mouse or other pointing device.
- An 800 x 600 resolution monitor.
- Network cards and cabling for local network access.
- Internet access (see your local network administrator).
- A printer (optional).
- A projection system to display the instructor's computer screen.

Software

- Either Windows XP Professional with Service Pack 1, or Windows 2000 Professional with Service Pack 4.
- Microsoft® Professional Edition 2003.

Class Setup

For Initial Class Setup

1. Install Windows 2000 Professional or Windows XP Professional on an empty partition.
    - Leave the Administrator password blank.
    - For all other installation parameters, use values that are appropriate for your environment (see your local network administrator for details).

2. On Windows 2000 Professional, when the Network Identification Wizard runs after installation, select the Users Must Enter A User Name And Password To Use This Computer option. (This step ensures that students will be able to log on as the Administrator user regardless of what other user accounts exist on the computer.)
3. On Windows 2000 Professional, in the Getting Started with Windows 2000 window, uncheck Show This Screen At Startup. Click Exit.
4. On Windows 2000 Professional, set 800 x 600 display resolution: Right-click the desktop and choose Properties. Select the Settings tab. Move the Screen Area slider to 800 By 600 Pixels. Click OK twice, then click Yes.
5. On Windows 2000 Professional, install Service Pack 4. Use the Service Pack installation defaults.
6. On Windows XP Professional, disable the Welcome screen. (This step ensures that students will be able to log on as the Administrator user regardless of what other user accounts exist on the computer.) Click Start and choose Control Panel→User Accounts. Click Change The Way Users Log On And Off. Uncheck Use Welcome Screen. Click Apply Options.
7. On Windows XP Professional, install Service Pack 1. Use the Service Pack installation defaults.
8. On either operating system, install a printer driver (a physical print device is optional).
   - For Windows XP Professional, click Start and choose Printers and Faxes. Under Printer Tasks, click Add A Printer and follow the prompts.
   - For Windows 2000 Professional, click Start and choose Settings→Printers. Run the Add Printer Wizard and follow the prompts.

   If you do not have a physical printer installed, right-click the printer and choose Pause Printing to prevent any print error messages.
9. On either operating system, verify that file extensions are visible.
   a. Right-click the Start menu button and choose Explore from the shortcut menu to open Windows Explorer.
   b. In Windows Explorer, choose Tools→Folder Options to open the Folder Options dialog box.
   c. In the Folder Options dialog box, select the View tab.
   d. If necessary, uncheck the Hide Extensions For Known File Types check box.
   e. Click Apply and click OK, and then close Windows Explorer.
10. Run the Internet Connection Wizard to set up the Internet connection as appropriate for your environment, if you did not do so during installation.
11. Log on to the computer as the Administrator user if you have not already done so.
12. Perform a Complete installation of Microsoft Office 2003 System.
13. Minimize the Language Bar, if necessary.
14. On the course CD-ROM, open the 084360 folder. Then, open the Data folder. Run the 084360dd.exe self-extracting file located within. This will install a folder named 084360Data on your C drive. This folder contains all the data files that you will use to complete this course.
15. Move all files and subfolders from 084360Data to the My Documents folder for the Administrator user.

Before Every Class

1. Log on to each computer as the Administrator user.
2. Delete any existing data files from the My Documents folder.
3. Extract a fresh copy of the course data files from the CD-ROM provided with the course manual and move all files and subfolders from 084360Data to the My Documents folder for the Administrator user.
4. Start Word.
5. Disable the Readability Statistics.
   a. Choose Tools→Options and select the Spelling & Grammar tab.
   b. If necessary, disable the Show Readability Statistics option and click OK.
6. Delete the Product Names.dic custom dictionary.
   a. On the Spelling And Grammar tab, click Custom Dictionaries.
   b. In the Custom Dictionaries dialog box, select Product Names.dic, click Remove, and click OK.
   c. Click Add to display the Add Custom Dictionary dialog box.
   d. In the list of files, select Product Names.dic, press Delete, and click Yes to confirm the deletion.
   e. To close the open dialog boxes, click Cancel, click OK, and click OK again.
7. Delete the "Burke Properties" AutoText entry.
   a. Choose Insert→AutoText→AutoText.
   b. In the AutoCorrect dialog box on the AutoText tab, select the "Burke Properties" entry in the list.
   c. Click Delete.
   d. Click OK to close the dialog box.
8. Reset the Results Should Be options in the Clip Art task pane to All Media Types.
   a. In the Clip Art task pane, display the Results Should Be drop-down list.
   b. Select All Media Types.
   c. To clear "money" from the search list, search for "house."
   d. Close the Clip Art task pane.
9. If you do not have a physical printer installed, clear the print queue for your installed printer: Open the Printers or Printers And Faxes window, right-click the printer, and choose Cancel All Documents. Click Yes. Close the window.

List of Additional Files

Printed with each activity is a list of files students open to complete that activity. Many activities also require additional files that students do not open, but are needed to support the file(s) students are working with. These supporting files are included with the student data files on the course CD-ROM or data disk. Do not delete these files.

NOTES

LESSON 1
Creating a Basic Document

Lesson Time
50 minutes

Lesson Objectives:

In this lesson, you will create a basic document.

You will:

- Identify the components of the Word 2003 environment.
- Get help using Word.
- Enter text.
- Save a document.
- Preview a document.
- Print a document.

Introduction

Perhaps you have been handwriting letters or using a typewriter to create your personal and business documents. Transitioning your correspondence to a computer program may seem a little daunting. Don't worry, though. In this lesson, you will create a basic document using Microsoft® Office Word 2003.

No matter what profession you are in, the process of learning something new requires that you gain some basic skills to perform even the most common tasks. Learning a new computer program is no different. Time spent familiarizing yourself with Word as you create a basic document will help you to acquire the fundamental skills you need to create more complex documents.

TOPIC A

The Word Environment

You have been assigned new responsibilities. To accomplish those responsibilities, you need to use Microsoft Word. In this topic, you will start Word and identify various components in the program window.

When you move to a new neighborhood, you typically want to look around—get a feel for the place, locate the nearest bank, post office, grocery store, and so on. Familiarizing yourself with where things are will make your life easier when you need to go somewhere or get something done. Using new software is no different. Looking around a new program's interface will help you prepare for when you need to begin using the program to do your work.

Microsoft® Office Word 2003

Microsoft Office Word 2003 is a program used to create, revise, and save documents for printing, distribution, or future retrieval. Word's tools can help you make your documents more accurate, concise, and correct.

The Microsoft® Office System is a collection of services and programs that work together to help you solve computing challenges.

Personalized Menus and Toolbars

Word's menus and toolbars adapt to how you use them. For instance, when you click a menu's name, Word displays an abbreviated version of the menu, called a *short menu*, which lists the most commonly used commands. To view the menu's less commonly used commands, display its *expanded menu* by clicking the downward-pointing Expand button located at the bottom of the short menu. To display less commonly used toolbar buttons, you need to click the Toolbar Options button .

To quickly expand a menu, double-click the menu name.

If you prefer to display full menus and/or to display the Standard and Formatting toolbars on two rows, choose Tools→Customize, and then select the Options tab and select the first two check boxes.

How Menus and Toolbars Adapt

As you use menu options, they will be promoted to the short version of the menu. Over time, if you don't use a command on the short menu, Word will demote the unused command to the expanded menu.

Explore Word

The program window in Word contains a wide variety of elements. Table 1-1 and Figure 1-1 identify many of the program's window elements.

Table 1-1: *Word Program Window Elements*

Item	Description
Title bar	Displays the name of the application and the name of the active document.
Menu bar	Lists the available program menu choices.
Type A Question For Help box	Provides quick access to help.
Close Window button	Closes the active document window.
Standard toolbar	Provides quick access to frequently used commands.
Formatting toolbar	Provides quick access to frequently used formatting commands.
Task pane	Provides easy access to commonly used commands. Different task panes display depending upon what you are doing.
Horizontal and vertical rulers	Provide ongoing page measurement as well as quick access to margins, tabs, and indents.
Text area	The area where documents are displayed and where you enter your document text.
Selection bar	An area in the left margin of a document used to select text.
Insertion point	Indicates where text will be inserted as you type.
Horizontal and vertical scroll bars	Display different areas of the active document.
View buttons	Change the document's view.
Status bar	Displays information about the active document, such as the current page number.

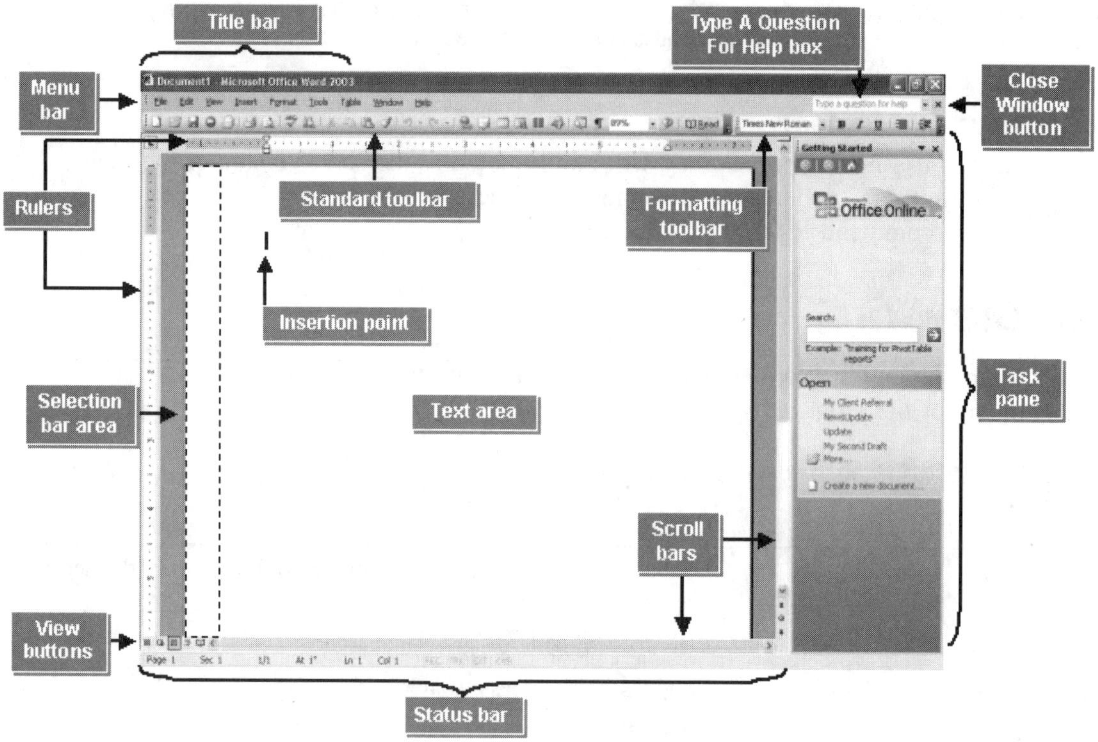

Figure 1-1: *The Microsoft Office Word 2003 program window.*

Mouse Pointers

As you use Word, you will notice that the mouse pointer changes shape depending on where it is located in the program window. Table 1-2 lists the common mouse pointers and their purposes.

Table 1-2: *Mouse Pointer Icons*

Location	Mouse Pointer	Used To
In the text area		Indicate the location of the mouse pointer.
Outside the text area		Select menu commands, toolbar buttons, and so on.
In the selection bar		Select lines, paragraphs, and the entire document.
In the task pane		Display more information.

ScreenTips

As you position the mouse pointer over items in the program window, such as toolbar buttons, Word may display a descriptive label. These labels are called *ScreenTips*. (See Figure 1-2.) Use them to identify program window items or to help you distinguish between similar looking items.

change default font - format - font - make changes - don't click ok but click default

to change margins file - page set up

tools - customize - options

to change most defaults - tools → options → general

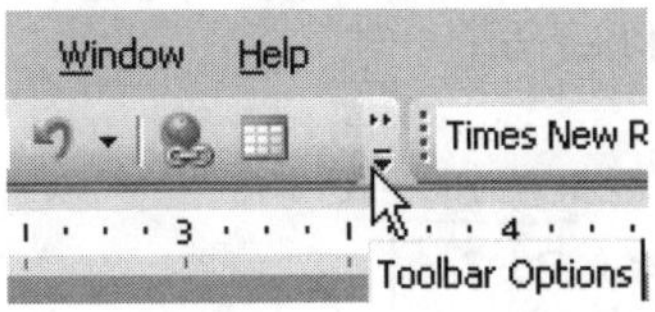

Figure 1-2: *A ScreenTip displays when you position the mouse pointer over a toolbar button.*

ACTIVITY 1-1

Exploring the Word Program Window

Setup:

Your computer is on and Word has been properly installed.

Scenario:

Your company just purchased and installed Microsoft Office Professional Edition 2003 software. Since your job responsibilities typically require you to use Microsoft Office Word 2003, you need to take some time to get to know the Word environment.

What You Do	How You Do It
1. **Start Word.**	a. From the taskbar, **click Start.** b. **Choose All Programs→Microsoft Office→Microsoft Office Word 2003.** If you are using Windows 2000, choose Programs→Microsoft Office→Microsoft Office Word 2003.
2. **Identify the various Microsoft Office Word 2003 program window elements.** Use Figure 1-1 as a reference.	
3. **Expand the Edit menu.**	a. In the Menu bar, **choose Edit.** The short menu is displayed by default.

b. At the bottom of the menu, **click the Expand button.**

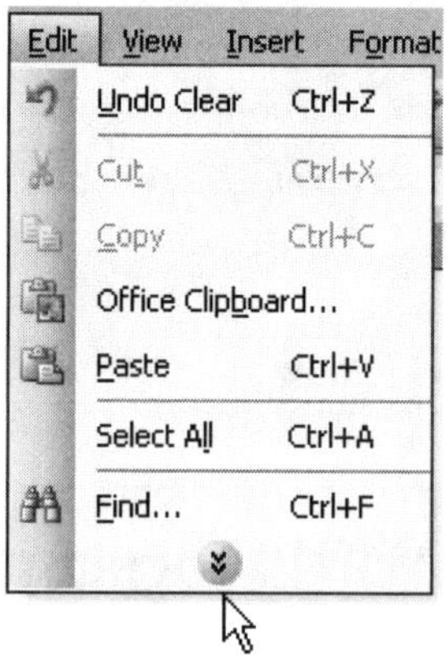

c. **Click away from the Edit menu** to close it.

4. **Display the available buttons for the Standard toolbar.**

a. On the Standard toolbar, **locate the Toolbar Options button.**

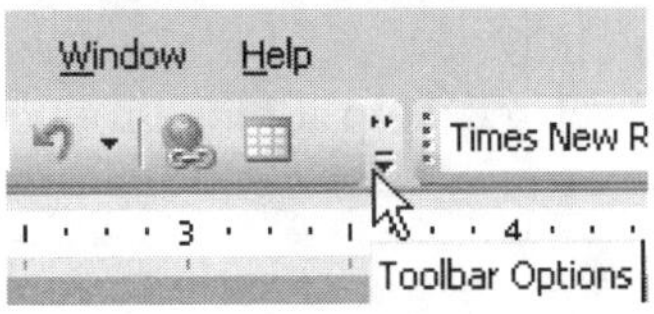

b. **Click the Toolbar Options button** to display the available buttons.

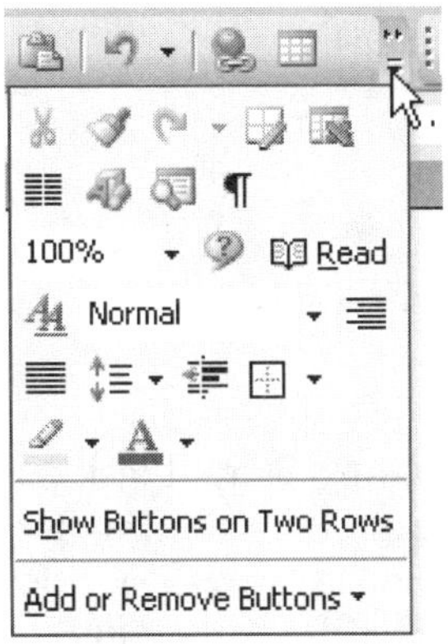

c. **Click away from the Toolbar Options button** to close it.

TOPIC B

Get Help Using Word

As you use Word, you may come across things that are unfamiliar to you. In this topic, you will use Word's built-in help system to get assistance when you have a question.

You may have once heard the phrase, "Physician, heal thyself." In Word, the counterpart would be, "Word user, help thyself." Although most of us aren't capable of healing ourselves, Word's built-in help system enables us to help ourselves whenever we have Word-related questions. As a result, you no longer need to rely on your co-workers or tech support. You can find the answers you need immediately. In short, the help system can increase your knowledge of Word as well as your independence.

Help Task Pane

The Help task pane provides you with a quick way to find answers to your questions. Another useful feature of the Help task pane is the Table Of Contents option, which contains a comprehensive list of Word-related help topics grouped by task. (See Figure 1-3.)

Figure 1-3: *The Help task pane.*

Show and Hide Task Panes

By default, the Getting Started task pane is displayed when you start Word. However, if you want to see more of the program window, you can hide the task pane area from view. To do so, choose View→Task Pane. If you want to display a specific task pane in the task pane area, from the Other Task Panes drop-down list, select the desired task pane. (See Figure 1-4.)

You can also quickly show or hide the task pane by pressing Ctrl+F1.

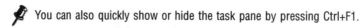

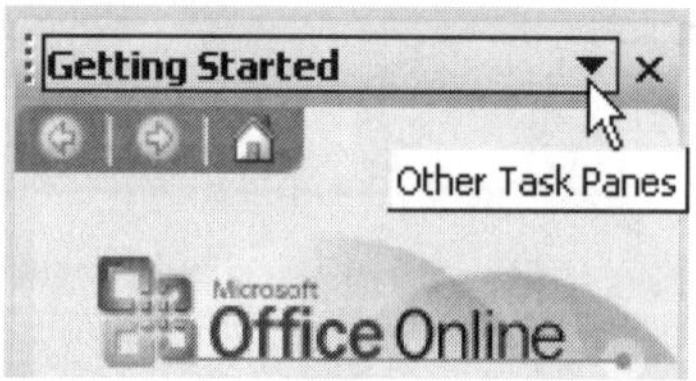

Figure 1-4: *Show any task pane using the Other Task Panes drop-down list.*

Additional Methods for Getting Help in Word

From the Help menu or in the lower half of the Help task pane, you may notice the Office Online options. These are several different ways to get help from online resources, such as access to additional training and/or online communities. Clicking any of the links in this area displays the Office-related help topics in a Web browser window. (The Help menu on the menu bar offers similar options.)

To take full advantage of Word's additional online offerings, you will need to have an active Internet connection.

Search Results Task Pane

Whenever you use the Type A Question For Help text box in the menu bar or any task pane to search for something, the results will be listed in the Search Results task pane. (See Figure 1-5.) When you click a result in the task pane, the related information is displayed in a Microsoft Office Word Help window.

Figure 1-5: *The Search Results task pane.*

How to Get Help Using Word

There are many ways to get help in Word, but the most common method is using the Type A Question For Help box.

Procedure Reference: Use the Type A Question For Help Box

To get help using the Type A Question For Help box:

1. Place the insertion point in the Type A Question For Help text box.

   You can also use the Word Help task pane. To display it, choose Help→Microsoft Office Word Help.

2. Type your question and press Enter. A list of results that may answer your question is displayed in the Search Results task pane.

   Previously asked questions are available in the Type A Question For Help drop-down list.

3. In the Search Results task pane, click the desired result to display the related help topic(s) in a Microsoft Office Word Help window.

ACTIVITY 1-2

Getting Help with Word

Setup:

Word is open with a new blank document displayed.

Scenario:

Since you are still a relatively new user of Word, you may want to learn more about how menus and toolbars work.

What You Do	How You Do It
1. **Use the Type A Question For Help box to learn more about how menus and toolbars work in Word.**	a. In the menu bar, **place the insertion point in the Type A Question For Help text box.** 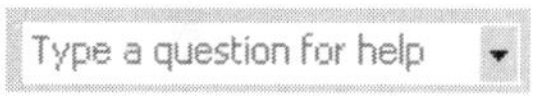
	b. **Type *How do menus and toolbars work?* and press Enter.**
	c. In the Search Results task pane, **click the About Menus And Toolbars result** to display the help topic.
2. **Display the definition for "menu."**	a. In the Microsoft Office Word Help window, **click the underlined word "menu"** to display its definition. 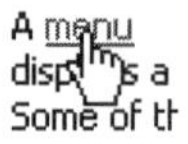 Clicking "menu" again hides the definition.

3. **Display all definitions and explanations on the About Menus And Toolbars screen.**

   a. Near the top of the About Menus And Toolbars screen, **click the underlined words "Show All."**

The "Show All" text turns to "Hide All."

   b. **Verify that all definitions and explanations have been displayed.**

4. **Close the Microsoft Office Word Help window.**

   a. In the upper-right corner of the Microsoft Office Word Help window, **click the Close button.**

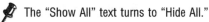

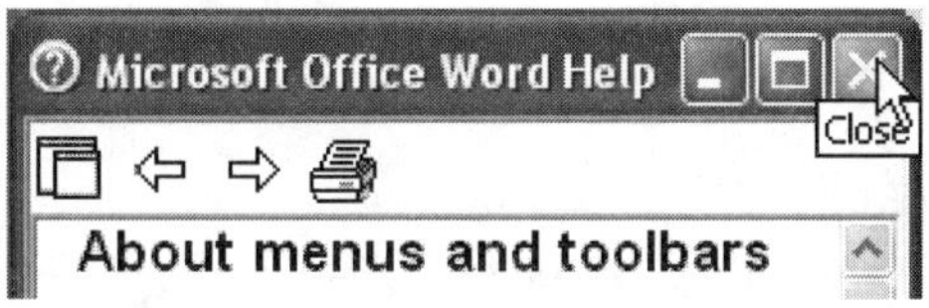

PRACTICE ACTIVITY 1-3

Using Help

Activity Time:

5 minutes

Scenario:

Although it's nice to know more about menus and toolbars, you have some topics in mind that you want to learn more about.

1. **Use the Type A Question For Help box to learn more about a topic of your choice.**

Suggested topics: getting help, shortcut keys, new features.

2. **Close any open Microsoft Office Word Help windows.**

Word's help system may launch a Microsoft Internet Explorer window to access help on the Web. If so, close the browser window.

3. **Close the Search Results task pane (choose View→Task Pane).**

TOPIC C

Enter Text

You have been asked to transcribe some handwritten notes into a document. To do that, you need to get text into a Word document. In this topic, you will enter text.

As you know, Word is a powerful word processor. However, with no words to process, the program does little more than take up room on your computer. The first step toward harnessing that power is to capture your ideas in a form that Word can use. Entering text into an open document is the way to do that.

New Blank Document

When you want to start a new document, click the New Blank Document button on the Standard toolbar. A new blank document is just what its name suggests: a new blank document containing basic page settings, such as margins, but no text or graphics.

You can also click Blank Document in the New Document task pane.

Formatting Marks

Definition:

Formatting marks are non-printing characters, such as spaces, paragraphs, and tabs, that are displayed in the text area. The marks act as placeholders and identify when a formatting key has been pressed. (See Figure 1-6.) To hide or show these formatting marks, you need to click the Show/Hide button ¶ on the Standard toolbar.

indent - press tab - every time 1/2"
if tab too far press back space

red squiggle - word not in dictionary
green squiggle grammer

Example:

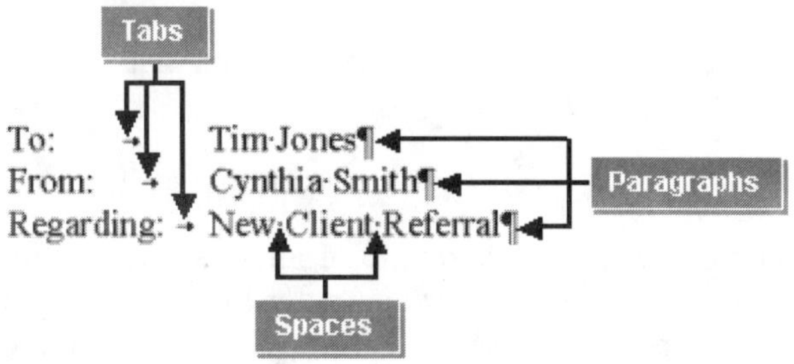

Figure 1-6: *Common non-printing formatting marks.*

Word Wrap

When you type, there's no need to manually end each line of text by pressing Enter. When the text nears the document's right margin, the text will automatically wrap to the beginning of the next line so that you can continue typing.

Default Typing Options

When you begin typing in a new blank document, you may notice that things happen automatically.

- AutoCorrect fixes common typographical errors, misspelled words, and incorrect capitalization.
- Smart tags are represented by a button  that is displayed in response to a given action, error, or automatic correction. Clicking a smart tag displays a list of options related to the action performed.
- Check Spelling And Grammar As You Type displays a wavy red underline or a wavy green underline below text that Word considers either a grammar or spelling mistake.
- AutoText inserts common or frequently used text, graphics, and other entries.

Disable Default Typing Options

Word's default typing options may be distracting or you may want to customize how they behave. You can change many of these options using the AutoCorrect dialog box (choose Tools→AutoCorrect Options). To selectively disable the spelling and grammar options, deselect the undesired options on the Spelling & Grammar tab in the Options dialog box (choose Tools→Options).

How to Enter Text

Procedure Reference: Enter Text in a New Document

To enter text:

1. If necessary, place the insertion point in the desired location.
2. Type the text you want to appear in the new document.
   - Press Enter to end a paragraph or to create a blank line between paragraphs.
   - Press Tab to indent the insertion point a half inch to the right.

Remember, Word will automatically wrap lines of text for you.

- Press Backspace to delete the character or space to the immediate left of the insertion point.
- Press Delete to delete the character or space to the immediate right of the insertion point.

Alternative Text Entry Methods

In addition to using the keyboard, Word offers a couple of alternative ways to enter text. With the proper equipment, you can train your computer to transcribe your spoken dictation or handwriting into typed text. Use the Help task pane to search for speech recognition or handwriting recognition for more details.

ACTIVITY 1-4

Entering Text in a New Document

Setup:

All Microsoft Office Word Help windows, Microsoft Internet Explorer browser windows, and the Search Results task pane are closed. A new blank document is displayed in Print Layout view.

Scenario:

You work for a real estate company named Burke Properties. You took a phone message for a client named Ms. Ellen Thomas. She's available to meet on the first of next month to discuss buying the Schyler house on Elm St. Since this location is outside your sales territory, you need to draft a client referral memo in Word to pass the client on to the appropriate agent, Tim Jones. When you are finished, your memo should be similar to the one shown in Figure 1-7.

Client·Referral·Memo¶
¶
To: → Tim·Jones¶
From:→Cindy·Smith¶
Re: → Client·Referral¶
¶
Ms.·Ellen·Thomas·wants·to·see·the·Schyler·house·in·your·territory.·(The·one·on·Elm·Street.)¶
¶
The·first·of·next·month·is·when·she·wants·to·meet.·Call·me·for·details.¶
¶
Yours·truly,¶
¶
Cindy¶

Figure 1-7: *Completed referral memo.*

What You Do	How You Do It
1. **Show the formatting marks.**	a. On the Standard toolbar, **click the Toolbar Options button** to display a list of available buttons.

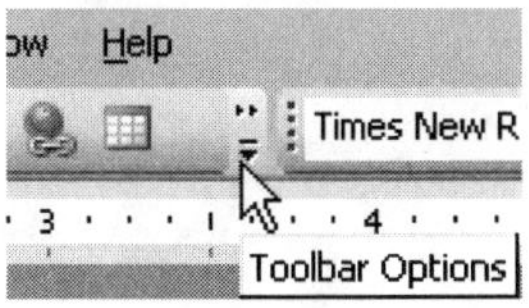

b. **Click the Show/Hide button** to display formatting marks.

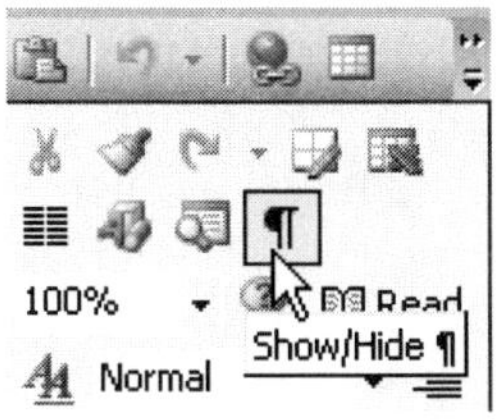

This also adds the Show/Hide button to the Standard toolbar.

2. **Complete the memo's heading information.** Use Figure 1-7 as a guide.

   a. **Type** ***Client Referral Memo*** **and press Enter** to end the paragraph.

   b. **Notice that Word displays space formatting marks between "Client," "Referral," and "Memo," as well as a new paragraph formatting mark when you press Enter.**

   c. **Press Enter** to add a blank line.

   d. **Type** ***To:***

   e. **Press Tab** to move the insertion point a half inch to the right and observe the formatting mark.

   f. **Type** ***Tim Jones*** **and press Enter.**

   g. **Type** ***From:*** **and press Tab.**

   h. **Type your first and last name and press Enter.**

   i. **Type** ***Re:*** **and press Tab.**

   j. **Type** ***Client Help***

---

3. **Replace the word "Help" with "Referral" and add a blank line.**

   a. **Press Backspace until the word "Help" is deleted.**

   b. **Type** ***Referral*** **and press Enter.**

   c. **Press Enter** to add a blank line after the reference line.

---

4. **Type the memo's first sentence.** Use Figure 1-7 as a guide.

   a. **Type** ***Ms. Ellen Thomas wants to see the Schyler house in your territory.***

---

5. **What do you notice about the word "Schyler"?**

---

6. **Type the memo's second sentence and add two blank lines.**

a. To begin a new sentence, **press the Spacebar.**

b. **Type *(The one on Elm Street.)***

c. **Press Enter twice.**

---

7. **What do you notice about the sentence "(The one on Elm Street.)"?**

---

8. To see how Word's AutoCorrect feature works, **intentionally misspell "the" as *teh*.**

a. **Type *teh* and stop.**

b. While observing the word, **press the Spacebar.**

---

9. **After typing "teh" and pressing the Spacebar, what was automatically corrected?**

a) The word was capitalized.

b) Nothing.

c) The word was marked as a grammatical error.

d) The misspelling was corrected.

e) The word was deleted.

---

10. **Display the AutoCorrect dialog box.**

a. **Move the mouse pointer just below the word "The"** to display the AutoCorrect Options smart tag.

b. **Click the smart tag** and observe the AutoCorrect Options menu.

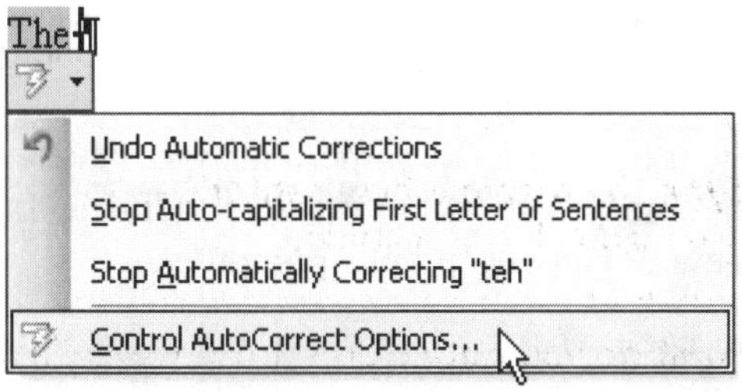

c. **Select Control AutoCorrect Options** to display the AutoCorrect tab in the AutoCorrect dialog box.

---

11. In the AutoCorrect dialog box, **locate the "teh" entry in the list of text that is replaced as you type.**	a. In the Replace Text As You Type area, in the Replace text box, **type *te*** to display the "teh" entry. b. **Click Cancel** to close the AutoCorrect dialog box.
12. **Type the rest of the memo's body text and add two blank lines.** Again, use Figure 1-7 as a guide.	a. **Reposition the insertion point after the word "The" and type *first of next month is when she wants to meet. Call me for details.*** b. **Press Enter twice.**
13. For the closing, **insert the "Yours truly," AutoText entry.**	a. **Type *Your*** 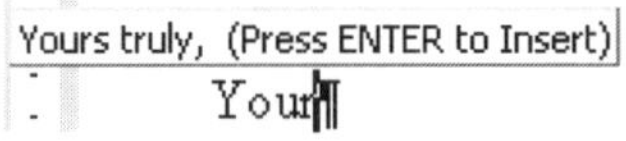 b. To insert the AutoText entry, **press Enter.**
14. **Finish the memo.**	a. **Press Enter twice.** b. **Type your first name.**

TOPIC D

Save a New Document

After you have entered some text, you may want to store the document so that it's accessible later in case you need to print or modify it. In this topic, you will learn how to save a copy of your new document to your computer.

You've been working late on an urgent report that your manager needs on her desk the first thing in the morning. You just finished writing it in Word. Though you are tired, you feel good because you know the report is great. Then, someone accidentally pulls your computer's power cord out of the wall. Where is your report now? If you saved it, it's still on your computer waiting for you when you restart. If you didn't save it, you may be out of luck. Saving a document early and often can prevent such mishaps.

Save Versus Save As

Word's Save command enables you to save an existing document with the same name in the same location. If you are saving a document for the first time, or if you want to change the name or location, you need to use the Save As command.

How to Save a Document

Procedure Reference: Save a New Document

To save a document for the first time, or with a different name, or to a different location:

1. Choose File→Save As to display the Save As dialog box.
2. Navigate to the location where you want to save the document.
   - Select a folder from the Save In drop-down list.
   - Or, click a folder in the My Places bar.
3. In the File Name text box, type the name of the file.
4. Click Save.

Document Naming Tips

When saving a document for the first time, by default Word assigns a file name by using the first words of your document. You can accept this default name or name it something different. When naming a document:

- Use a name that somehow describes the document's contents.
- Keep the descriptive name as short as possible.
- Avoid using any punctuation in your document name.

Procedure Reference: Create a New Folder

To create a new folder in the Save As dialog box:

You can also create a new folder in the Open dialog box.

1. On the Save As dialog box toolbar, click the Create New Folder button  .
2. In the Name text box, type a name for the new folder.
3. Click OK.

Procedure Reference: Save an Existing Document

To save changes to an existing document:

1. Save the document.
   - On the Standard toolbar, click the Save button  .
   - Choose File→Save.
   - Or, press Ctrl+S.

ACTIVITY 1-5

Saving a Document

Setup:

The newly created memo is complete and displayed.

Scenario:

You've been working on your client referral memo, but have just been called into your manager's office for an impromptu meeting. Rather than risk losing all the text that you've typed, you want to save your work. And because you know that this is the first of many referral memos you are likely to write, you want to save the document as My Client Referral in a new folder called My Referrals located in your My Documents folder.

What You Do	How You Do It
1. **In the title bar, the file name __________ indicates that the document has not been saved yet.**	
2. **Display the Save As dialog box.**	a. To display the Save As dialog box, **choose File→Save As.**
3. In the My Documents folder, **create a new folder called *My Referrals***	a. **Click the Create New Folder button**  **.** b. In the Name text box, **type *My Referrals*** 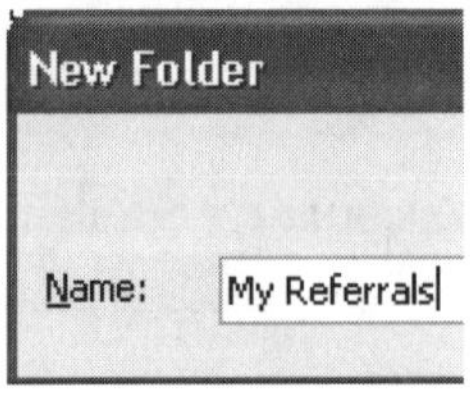 c. **Click OK** to display the new folder in the Save In drop-down list box.
4. **Save the file as *My Client Referral Memo*.**	a. In the File Name text box, **type *My Client Referral Memo*** 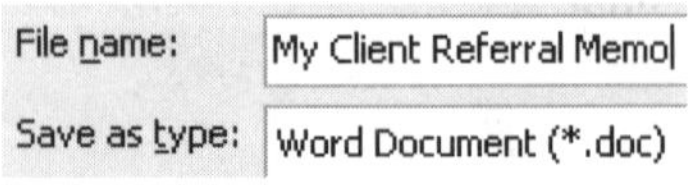 b. **Click Save.**

5. **You can tell that the file has been saved because the new file name is displayed in the______.**

TOPIC E

Preview a Document

The next logical step might be to print the file. However, before you do that, it's smart to preview the document so you can see what it might look like when printed. In this topic, you will preview your document.

Whether you realize it or not, printing a document costs money. Each page may cost only a few cents for paper and ink, but those pennies add up quickly if you are repeatedly printing a 20-page document, just to see how it will look on paper or to do a quick hard copy edit. By previewing your document before printing, you can still see how it will look and identify obvious errors without wasting money and the time it takes to print additional copies.

Print Preview Options

When a document is displayed in Print Preview, you have several ways to view the document. These options can be accessed from the Print Preview toolbar. (Figure 1-8 and Table 1-3 identify many of the toolbar's elements.)

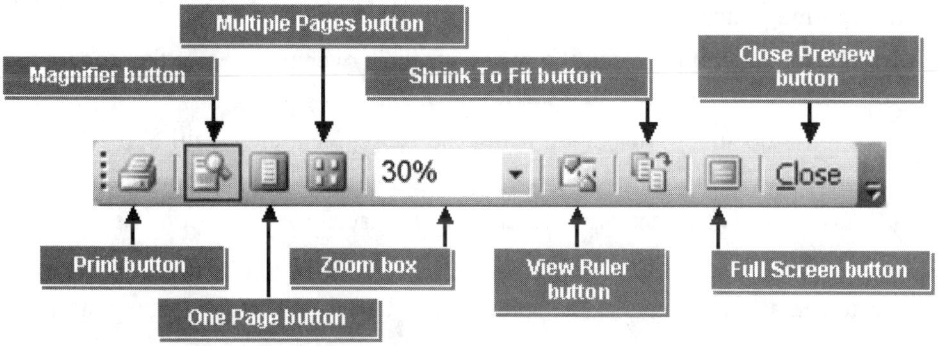

Figure 1-8: *The Print Preview toolbar.*

Table 1-3 explains the Print Preview toolbar buttons in detail.

Table 1-3: *Print Preview Toolbar Options*

Print Preview Toolbar Button	Description
	Sends the document directly to the default printer.
	Magnifies the document at 100% or zooms out to display one page or multiple pages.
	Displays an entire page.
	Displays more than one page at a time.

Print Preview Toolbar Button	Description
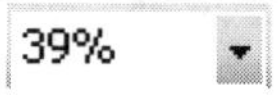	Displays a list of preset zoom settings or lets you enter a specific percentage.
	Hides and shows the horizontal and vertical rulers.
	Attempts to reduce the number of pages that will print.
	Hides the title bar, menu bar, status bar, and scroll bars.
	Closes Print Preview and redisplays the document in the previous view.

How to Preview a Document

Procedure Reference: Preview a Document

To preview a document:

1. Display the Preview window.
   - On the Standard toolbar, click the Print Preview button  .
   - Choose File→Print Preview.
   - Or, press Ctrl+F2.
2. Preview the document.
   - To use the Zoom tool, display the Zoom drop-down list and select the desired magnification.
   - To use the Magnifier, place the mouse pointer over the area in the document you want to see at 100% and click once.
   - To see the document displayed using the full screen, click Full Screen.

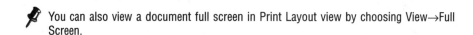

     You can also view a document full screen in Print Layout view by choosing View→Full Screen.
   - Or, to see several pages at the same time, click the Multiple Pages button.
3. On the Print Preview toolbar, click the Close button to return to Print Layout view.

ACTIVITY 1-6

Previewing a Document

Setup:

My Client Referral Memo is displayed.

Scenario:

You've returned from a meeting and Tim Jones was there. You told him about the memo that you were working on and he asked for a printed copy. Before you do that, however, you want to preview the document to identify any obvious errors. No sense in printing a copy with mistakes.

What You Do	How You Do It
1. **Preview My Client Referral Memo.**	a. On the Standard toolbar, **click the Print Preview button**. The Magnifier tool is active by default.
2. **Increase the memo's magnification to 50%.**	a. **Display the Zoom drop-down list.** b. **Select 50%.** 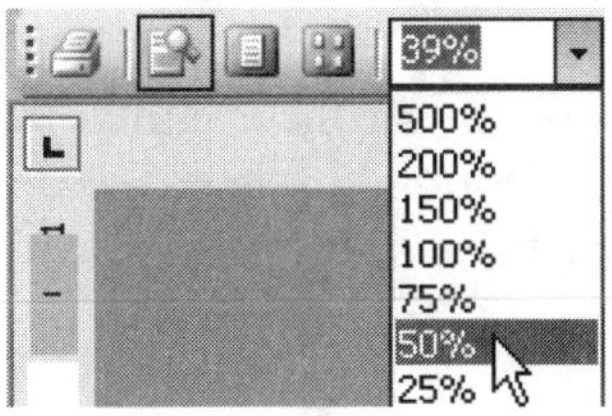 The text is still too small to read easily.
3. **Use the Magnifier to increase the magnification of the memo text.**	a. **Place the Magnifier over the top-left corner of the document.** b. To display the text at 100%, **click the mouse button once.**

4. **True or False? In Print Preview, you can see formatting marks, as well as spelling and grammar marks?**

__ True

__ False

5. Everything in the memo looks correct. **Close the Preview.**

a. On the Print Preview toolbar, **click the Close button** to redisplay the memo in Print Layout view.

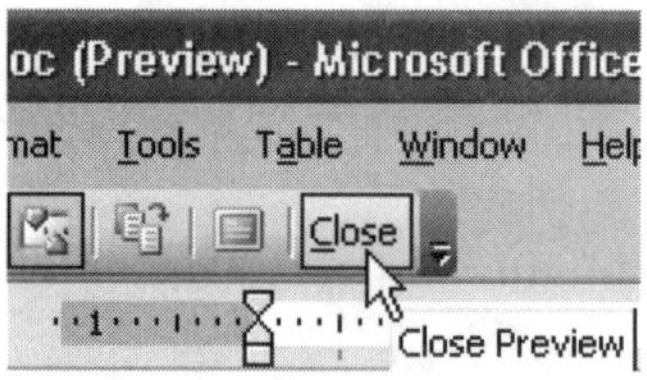

TOPIC F

Print a Document

Once you are satisfied with how your document looks when you preview it, you are ready to print the document. You will do that in this topic.

You and your manager are writing a contract that must be delivered across town by 5 PM or your company could lose millions of dollars. You printed a copy for your records and are about to email the contract when the power goes off. Your manager rushes into your office, but you calmly hand her a copy of the contract that you printed just moments ago. The printed contract can be sent by courier to meet the deadline. Technical problems often prevent delivery and distribution of documents. Printing provides a tangible hard copy that's easy to file, distribute, and read.

Print Options

You can print a document with the default print options by clicking the Print button on either the Print Preview or Standard toolbar. However, if you want to change any print options, you use the Print dialog box. Figure 1-9 and Table 1-4 identify many of these options.

File
↓
Print (will get dialog box)
can only reprint page desired
If hit print icon— will print all pages

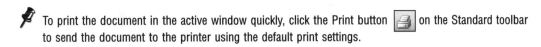

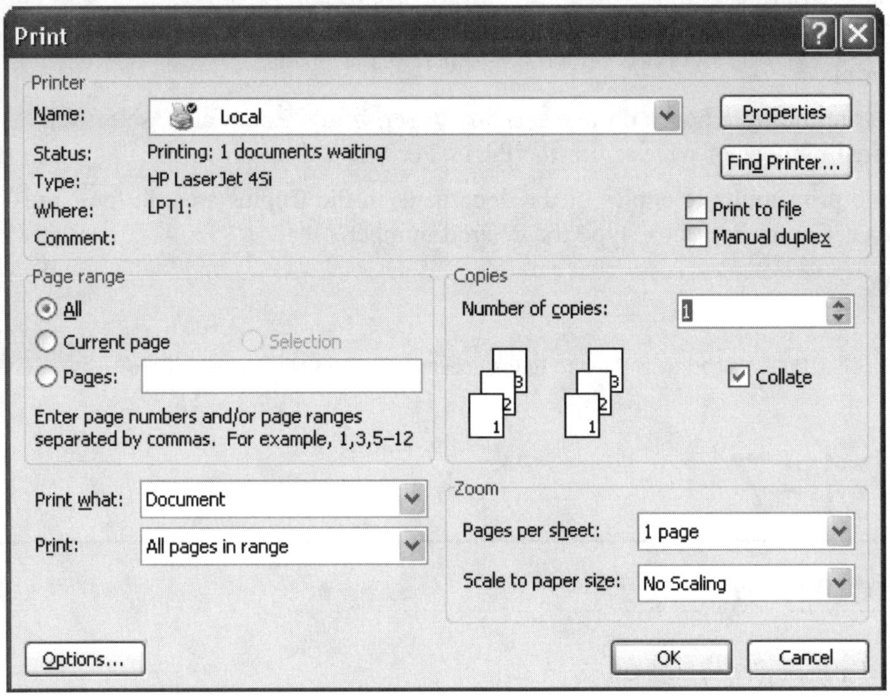

Figure 1-9: *The Print dialog box.*

Table 1-4: *Print Dialog Box Options*

Print Dialog Box Area	Description
Printer	You can select a different printer, display printer properties, and display the selected printer's status.
Page Range	You can specify exactly which pages you want to print.
Print What	You can print the document itself or other document attributes, such as its properties or AutoText entries.
Copies	You can select the number of copies you want and whether or not they are to be collated.
Zoom	Save paper by specifying how many pages will be printed on a single sheet of paper.

How to Print a Document

Procedure Reference: Print a Document

To print the document in the active window:

To print the document in the active window quickly, click the Print button on the Standard toolbar to send the document to the printer using the default print settings.

1. Display the Print dialog box.
   - Choose File→Print.
   - Or, press Ctrl+P.

2. Set the desired print options.
   - To print specific pages, under Page Range, type the page number(s) you want to print.
   - To print multiple pages on one sheet of paper, in the Zoom area, select the desired number of pages from the Pages Per Sheet drop-down list.
   - Or, to print multiple copies of the document, in the Copies area, in the Number Of Copies spin box, type the desired number.
3. Click OK.

To close the Print dialog box and return to the document without printing, click Cancel.

ACTIVITY 1-7

Printing a Document

Setup:

My Client Referral Memo is displayed.

Scenario:

Having previewed your memo, and being satisfied with how it looks and that there are no glaring errors, you need to print two copies: one for Tim Jones and one that you will submit to payroll later, so you receive the referral bonus.

What You Do	How You Do It
1. **Display the Print dialog box.** Do not click the Print button on the Standard toolbar. It does not display the Print dialog box.	a. **Choose File→Print** to display the Print dialog box.
2. **What print options might you use at your office? Why?**	

3. **Print two copies of the memo.**

a. Under Copies, in the Number Of Copies spin box, **type *2***

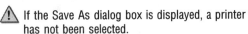

b. Leaving all of the other print options with their current settings, **click OK.**

If the Save As dialog box is displayed, a printer has not been selected.

---

4. **Close the memo.**

a. **Choose File→Close.**

b. If prompted to save changes, **click No.**

Lesson 1 Follow-up

In this lesson, you explored the Word environment and used Help to learn about a topic of interest. You also were introduced to some of Word's default typing options, such as AutoComplete, AutoCorrect, and AutoText, as you created a basic business document. Once you saved your document you viewed it using Print Preview just before you printed it. In the next lesson, you will learn some useful ways to edit your documents.

1. **What are some types of documents you will create in Word?**

2. **What do you think about Word's default typing options? Do you think they're useful or annoying?**

Notes

LESSON 2
Editing a Document

Lesson Time
1 hour(s)

Lesson Objectives:

In this lesson, you will edit documents by locating and modifying text.

You will:

- Navigate in a document.
- Insert text in an existing sentence.
- Select text in a document.
- Create an AutoText entry.
- Move and copy text from one location to another.
- Delete blocks of text.
- Undo changes made to a document.
- Find and replace text.

Introduction

You've learned how to create a new document. At some point you may need to revise it. In this lesson, you will make changes to your documents.

Editing a handwritten document requires you to rewrite the entire document to include the changes. Word minimizes the effort required to revise your documents by enabling you to change your existing documents at anytime, without using messy correction fluid and without starting your document over again.

TOPIC A

Navigate in a Document

After you have created a document, you may need to make changes to it. To do so, you need to be able to move around in the document to locate where the changes need to be made. This topic will prepare you to do just that.

You've been asked to make some simple changes to a list of instructions. Each list item needs the proper end punctuation. You could move the insertion point using the mouse every time, but each time that requires you to take your hand off the keyboard to use the mouse. You then have to move your hand back to the keyboard to type the change. That may not sound like a big deal—it only takes a few seconds—but over the course of a day, those seconds can add up to several minutes. Using the most appropriate navigation techniques in a document may save you an hour or two every week.

Open a Document

Procedure Reference: Open a Document

To open an existing document in Word:

1. Display the Open dialog box.
    - On the Standard toolbar, click the Open button  .
    - Choose File→Open.
    - Press Ctrl+O.
    - Or, in the Open section of the Home task pane, click More.

    Both the File menu and the Open section of the Home task pane contain a Recently Used File List, granting one-click access to the last four documents opened.

2. Navigate to the folder where the file is saved, using the My Places bar or the Look In drop-down list.
3. Select the document you want to open.

    If you want to see a document before opening it, in the Open dialog box, select the document and from the Views button's drop-down list, select Preview.

4. Click Open.

You can also double-click a file name in the Open dialog box to open the document.

The Open Dialog Box

The Open dialog box has a variety of ways to locate, manage, and open files. Figure 2-1 will help you locate the different items in the Open dialog box.

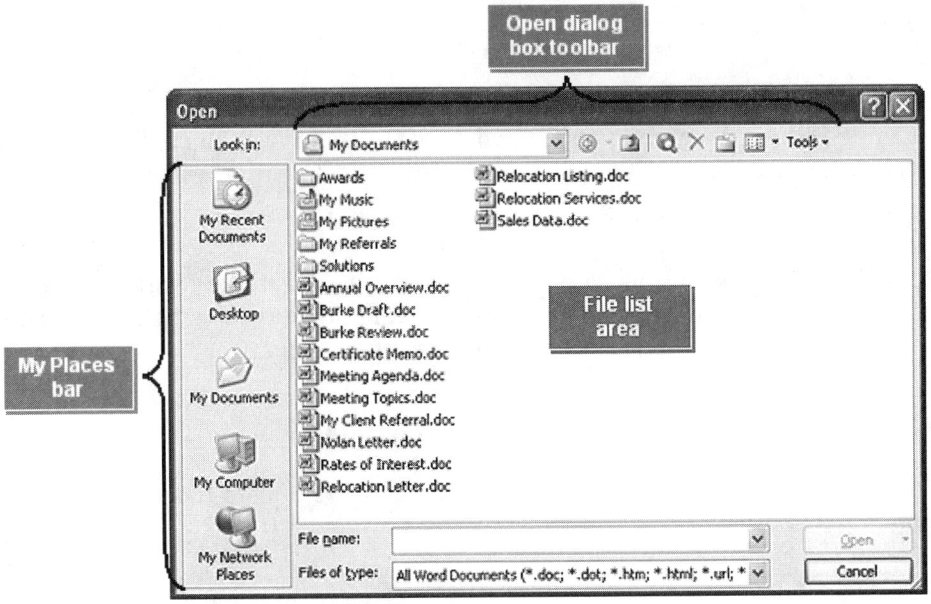

Figure 2-1: *The Open dialog box.*

Views in the Open Dialog Box

Sometimes it's difficult to tell one document from another in the Open dialog box based on just their names. The Views button  on the Open dialog box toolbar offers several ways to display more information about a document. Table 2-1 describes the views used for documents in greater detail.

Table 2-1: *Common Document Views in the Open Dialog Box*

View	Description
List	A list of the document names in the selected folder. This is the default view.
Details	The document name, size, type, and modification date for all files in the selected folder.
Properties	Summary information about a selected file, such as who authored it and when it was created.
Preview	A preview of a selected document on the right side of the Open dialog box.

ACTIVITY 2-1

Opening a Document

Data Files:

- Burke Draft.doc

Setup:

Word is running with no documents open. Student data files have been copied to the hard drive in the My Documents folder.

Scenario:

You have been asked to make some edits to a document named Burke Draft stored in the My Documents folder—the document contains background information about Burke Properties. You also need to verify that you are opening the correct document.

What You Do	How You Do It
1. **Display the contents of the My Documents folder.**	a. On the Standard toolbar, **click the Open button**.
	b. In the My Places bar, **click My Documents.**

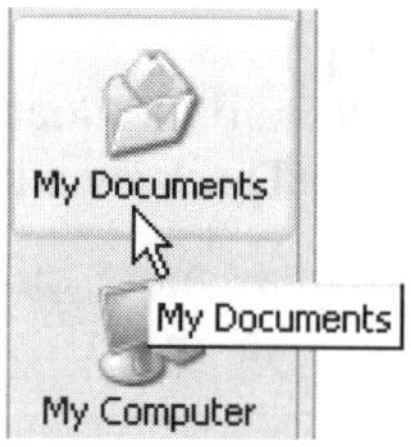

By default, all files are displayed in List view.

You could also click the Up One Level button.

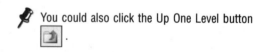

What You Do	How You Do It
2. In the Open dialog box, **preview Burke Draft.**	a. In the list of files, if necessary, **select Burke Draft.**

b. To display the Views button's drop-down list, **click the Views button's drop-down list arrow.**

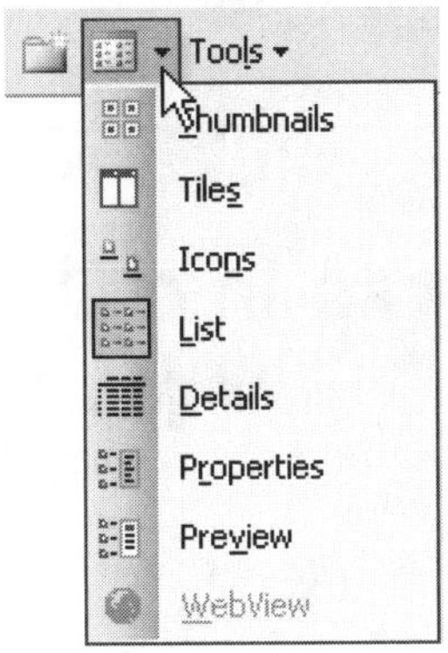

Repeatedly clicking the Views button in the Open dialog box cycles through the available views.

c. **Select Preview.** The document does start with "DRAFT."

d. **Use the Views button to return the view to List.**

---

3. **Open Burke Draft.**

a. In the file list, **select Burke Draft.**

b. **Click Open.**

Troubleshooting Opening Documents

Occasionally, you may have trouble opening a document. Often there are ways to overcome these problems. (See Table 2-2.)

Table 2-2: *Common Problems Associated with Opening Word Documents*

Problem	How to Fix
Word document doesn't have a file extension. (Rare, but has been known to happen.)	In Windows Explorer, rename the file so it has a .doc file extension.
Document was created by a program other than Word.	Open the file in the original program and change the Save As Type to Word Document (*.doc), Rich Text Format (*.rtf), or Plain Text (*.txt).
Document is already open. (Common when documents are stored on a network.)	Close the open document.
Document is protected. (Some documents may have security measures applied to them.)	You would need to request access to open the document.

Problem	How to Fix
Document has moved.	Navigate to new location and open the document.
Document is corrupt.	Re-create the document.

How to Navigate in a Document

You can use the vertical scroll bar to quickly view another part of a document. (See Table 2-3.) Navigating with the scroll bar does *not* change the position of the insertion point.

Table 2-3: *Navigation Techniques: Vertical Scroll Bar*

When You	The View Changes By
Click the scroll up or scroll down arrow	Scrolling up or down one line at a time.
Drag the scroll box to the top, bottom, or middle of the scroll bar	Displaying the top, bottom, or middle of a document.
Click in the shaded area above or below the scroll box	Scrolling the document up or down one screen at a time.

To move the insertion point in an open document, you can use a variety of keys. (See Table 2-4.) Using the keyboard, you change what is displayed on the screen as well as the position of the insertion point. The insertion point's current location is always reflected in the status bar at the bottom of the program window.

Table 2-4: *Navigation Techniques: Keyboard Shortcuts*

Press the	To Move the Insertion Point
Right Arrow	One space to the right.
Left Arrow	One space to the left.
Ctrl+Right Arrow	One word to the right.
Ctrl+Left Arrow	One word to the left.
Down Arrow	One line down.
Up Arrow	One line up.
Ctrl+Down Arrow	One paragraph down.
Ctrl+Up Arrow	One paragraph up.
Page Down	Down one screen.
Page Up	Up one screen.
Ctrl+Page Down	To the top of the next page.
Ctrl+Page Up	To the top of the previous page.
End	To the end of a line.
Home	To the beginning of a line.
Ctrl+End	To the end of the document.
Ctrl+Home	To the top of the document.

double arrow up or down on rt. handside

move up or down whole page of document

DISCOVERY ACTIVITY 2-2

Navigating in an Open Document

Setup:

Burke Draft is open.

Scenario:

You want to get an idea of what you are in for before you begin editing the document. You decide to look over the document to find out how long it is and to review its content. (Use the techniques shown in Table 2-3 and Table 2-4.)

1. **By default, when a document is opened, the insertion point is located at the___ of the document.**

2. **Display different parts of the document using the vertical scroll bar.** (See Table 2-3 for scroll-bar navigation techniques.) **As you scroll, be sure to keep an eye on the status bar information.**

   As you drag the scroll box, you may notice a ScreenTip with the number of the current page being displayed.

3. **As you scrolled, what information in the status bar changed?**

4. **As you scrolled, did the location of the insertion point change? How can you tell?**

5. **Move the insertion point to different parts of the document using keyboard shortcuts.** (See Table 2-4 for keyboard shortcut navigation techniques.) **As you move the insertion point, be sure to keep an eye on the status bar information.**

6. **As you used keyboard navigation techniques, did the location of the insertion point change? How can you tell?**

7. **How many pages are in the document?_**

TOPIC B

Insert Text

Once you know how to navigate within a document, it's time to put that knowledge to use. In this topic, you will navigate to a specified location to insert new text.

You want your document's meaning to be as clear as possible. That's not always the case after typing a first draft. As you enter text, often you type the words as they come to mind. Once you've had a chance to review a printed copy of the document, chances are good that you will want to add small amounts of text, a word here and there, just to clarify the message you are trying to convey.

How to Insert Text

Procedure Reference: Insert Text in a Document

To insert text:

1. Place the insertion point at the location where you want to insert new text.

   Press Insert to overtype existing text to the right of the insertion point.

2. Type the new text that you want to appear in the document.

Line Breaks

A *line break* is displayed as a formatting mark and is used to end the current line before it wraps to the next line automatically without starting a new paragraph. When formatting marks are displayed, the line break looks like this ↵ in the text area.

Procedure Reference: Insert a Line Break

To insert a line break:

1. Place the insertion point at the location where you want to insert the line break.
2. Press Shift+Enter to force a line to break while still remaining part of the paragraph.

ACTIVITY 2-3

Inserting Text in an Open Document

Setup:

Burke Draft is open, formatting marks are displayed, and the insertion point is at the top of the document.

If you accidentally changed the document in the previous activity, close it without saving changes and open it again. You will need a clean copy of the file for the next activity.

Scenario:

After reviewing the Burke Draft document, you decide to clarify two things. Near the end of the document, "New York, New Jersey, and Pennsylvania" is the only three-state grouping in the list. It needs to refer to these states as "The Tri-State Area." Also, you want to mark the modified document as a second draft.

What You Do	How You Do It
1. On page 3, before "New York, New Jersey, and Pennsylvania," **insert *The Tri-State Area (*.**	a. On page 3, **place the insertion point before the "N" in "New York..."** ¶ New·York,·New·Jersey,·Pennsylvania¶ b. **Type *The Tri-State Area (***
2. **Insert a close parenthesis after "Pennsylvania."** ·Pennsylvania)¶	a. To move the insertion point to the end of the line, **press End.** b. **Type *)***
3. Since text now spans more than half the page, **insert a line break so the parenthetical text is on its own line.** Tri-State·Area·↵ (New·York,·New·Jersey,·Pennsylvania)¶	a. **Place the insertion point before the open parenthesis.** Tri-State·Area·(New· b. To insert a line break, **press Shift+Enter.**

4. At the top of the document, before the word "DRAFT" **insert the word *SECOND*.**

   a. To move the insertion point to the beginning of the document, **press Ctrl+Home.**

   b. **Type *SECOND* in all capital letters.**

   c. To separate the words with a space, **press the Spacebar.**

   SECOND DRAFT—Burke

5. **Save the document as *My Second Draft* in the My Documents folder.**

   a. To rename an existing document with a new name, **choose File→Save As.**

   b. In the File Name drop-down list box, **type *My Second Draft***

   c. **Click Save.**

TOPIC C

Select Text

Once you have your text in a document, you may want to make some more extensive edits. But before you can perform most editing techniques in Word, you need to first select the text you want to edit. In this topic, you will select text.

Without being able to select text, the number of things you can do in Word will be limited. You need to be able to select text to take advantage of the program's more powerful word processing capabilities without spending a lot of time.

How to Select Text

If you want to change text, you have to select it first. Using the mouse and keyboard, you can select individual characters, words, sentences, paragraphs, and entire documents.

Many keyboard navigation shortcuts can be combined with Shift to select text.

Table 2-5 shows the most common selection techniques.

Table 2-5: *Text Selection Techniques*

Selection Method	How to Make the Selection
Drag	Place the insertion point at one end of the text you want to select. Press and hold the mouse button. Move the mouse pointer to the other end of the text; this creates a highlighted area (a selection) between the two ends. Then release the mouse button. This method is ideal for small selections, such as individual characters.
Select a word	Place the mouse pointer over the word you want to select and double-click the mouse button. Word selects the trailing space along with the word, but not punctuation marks.
Select a sentence	Place the mouse pointer over the sentence you want to select. While pressing Ctrl, click the mouse button. Word selects end punctuation and trailing spaces along with the sentence.
Select a line	Place the mouse pointer over in the selection bar next to the line you want to select. The mouse pointer will change from an I-beam to a right-pointing arrow. Click the mouse button and Word selects the entire line of text.
Select multiple lines	Place the mouse pointer in the selection bar next to the first or last line of text you want to select. Press and hold the mouse button, and drag down or up to select additional lines.
Select a paragraph	Place the mouse pointer over the paragraph you want to select and triple-click the mouse button. Word automatically selects the paragraph mark along with the paragraph.
Select a document	Place the mouse pointer over the selection bar and, while pressing Ctrl, click the mouse button, or point in the selection bar and triple-click. (You can also choose Edit→Select All, or press Ctrl+A.)
Select a variable amount of text	Place the insertion point at the beginning of the text you want to select. While pressing Shift, press the desired Arrow keys to select just the text you want.
Extend a selection	Make a selection. While pressing Shift, press the Right Arrow key to extend the selection one character at a time, or press the Down Arrow key to extend the selection one line at a time.
Shorten a selection	Make a selection. While pressing Shift, press the Left Arrow key to shorten the selection one character at a time, or press the Up Arrow key to shorten the selection one line at a time.
Select items that aren't next to each other	Select the first item (a line or paragraph, for example), press and hold Ctrl, and use the mouse to select any additional items you want.
Deselect	Make another selection, or click the mouse button anywhere in the text area away from the selected text.

ACTIVITY 2-4

Selecting Text in an Open Document

Setup:

My Second Draft is open.

Scenario:

In order to edit documents efficiently, you must be able to select the text you want to affect. You decide to practice various text selection techniques in the open document.

What You Do	How You Do It
1. **Select the words "SECOND DRAFT."**	a. **Place the insertion point before the "S" in "SECOND."**
	b. **Press and hold the mouse button as you drag the mouse pointer so that both "SECOND" and "DRAFT" are highlighted.**
	c. To complete the selection, **release the mouse button.**
2. In the paragraph that begins with "Burke Properties was founded...," **select the first line.**	a. To the left of the line that begins with "Burke Properties was founded...," **position the mouse pointer in the selection bar.**
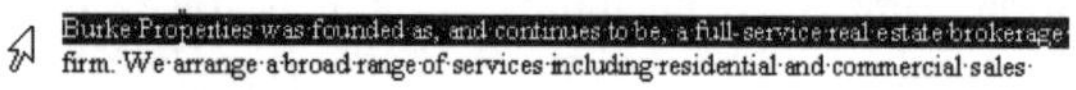	b. To select the entire line, **click the mouse button once.**
3. **Use the Shift and Right Arrow keys to extend the selection so it includes "firm."**	a. **As you press and hold Shift, press the Right Arrow five times** to select the word "firm" and the end punctuation.
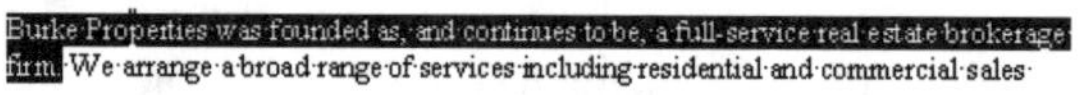	b. **Release the Shift key.**
4. **Select the "Burke Properties was founded..." paragraph.**	a. **Place the mouse pointer over the "Burke Properties was founded..." paragraph.**
	b. **Click the mouse button three times quickly** to select the paragraph.
5. **Select all the text in the document.**	a. **Choose Edit→Select All.**

6.	**Deselect the document text.**	a.	**Click the mouse button anywhere in the text area** to cancel the selection.

7. **What happens to text when you select it?**

8. **Do you find selecting text easier using the mouse, the keyboard, or a combination of both?**

TOPIC D

Create an AutoText Entry

Inserting text is great for adding a new word or two to a document. However, if you want to insert commonly repeated items that rarely change, like a legal disclaimer, Word can help there too. In this topic, you will create an AutoText entry.

AutoText can save you from typing the same text over and over, while ensuring that the text is consistently inserted into your documents each and every time. For instance, when you send out a business letter, you end it by typing your name, job title, and company contact information. Rather than typing the same closing each time, and potentially making typing mistakes or forgetting to include contact details, you can type the closing once and store it as an AutoText entry. Then, the next time you type a letter, you can simply insert your AutoText closing with just a few keystrokes.

AutoText

AutoText is a way to store and enter commonly or frequently used text, graphics, or tables. Each item is stored with a unique name and can be used repeatedly to enter items in a document with just a few keystrokes. Figure 2-2 shows some of the AutoText entries that come with Word.

Word comes with a wide variety of AutoText entries you can use right away.

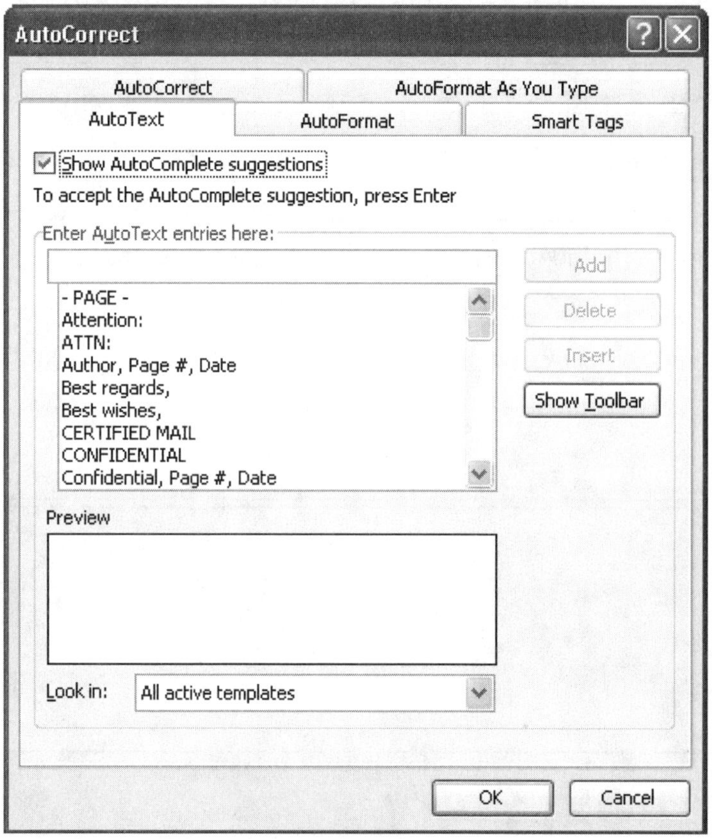

Figure 2-2: *The AutoText tab in the AutoCorrect dialog box.*

AutoText Versus AutoCorrect

Because AutoText and AutoCorrect sound similar and the fact that they can be used to achieve similar results, the difference between them can be a little confusing. To simplify the distinction between the two, use AutoText whenever your intention is to save time entering text, graphics, or tables. Use AutoCorrect whenever your intention is to have Word automatically fix common typing mistakes.

How to Create an AutoText Entry

Procedure Reference: Create an AutoText Entry

To create a new AutoText entry:

1. Locate the text, graphics, or table you want included in the AutoText entry.
2. Select the desired information.
3. Display the Create AutoText dialog box.
   - Choose Insert→AutoText→New.
   - Or press Alt+F3.

   By default, the new AutoText entry name matches the first two words in the selected text.
4. In the Please Name Your AutoText Entry text box, type the name for your new entry.

AutoText entry names must be unique and at least four characters long if you want to use AutoComplete to insert them in your documents.

5. Click OK to create the entry and to close the Create AutoText dialog box.

Procedure Reference: Insert an AutoText Entry

To insert an existing AutoText entry in a document:

1. Place the insertion point where you want the AutoText entry to be inserted.
2. Insert the AutoText entry.
   - Type the first four characters of the entry name and press Enter. (This method uses AutoComplete.)
   - Choose Insert→AutoText. Select the appropriate category submenu and select the desired AutoText entry. Custom entries are listed on the Normal submenu.

     You can also use the AutoText toolbar. (Choose View→Toolbars→AutoText.)

   - Or choose Insert→AutoText→AutoText. Select the desired AutoText entry and click Insert.

You can also use the AutoText toolbar. (Choose View→Toolbars→AutoText.)

Procedure Reference: Delete an AutoText Entry

To delete an AutoText entry:

1. Choose Insert→AutoText→AutoText to display the AutoText tab in the AutoCorrect dialog box.
2. In the Enter AutoText Entries Here list, select the AutoText entry you want to delete.
3. Click Delete.
4. Click OK.

Redefine an AutoText Entry

If you try to create a new AutoText entry with the same name as an existing AutoText entry, you will be prompted with a dialog box asking, "Do you want to redefine the AutoText entry?" If you click Yes, you will replace the existing entry with the new one. This is a useful method for updating existing AutoText entries.

ACTIVITY 2-5

Creating and Using an AutoText Entry

Setup:

My Second Draft is open and all text has been deselected.

Scenario:

You type Burke Properties dozens of times each day in different Word documents. To save some keystrokes, you want to create an AutoText entry for your company name. As you reviewed the draft document, you noticed that the list of locations isn't clearly identified as Burke Properties locations. You can use your AutoText entry to fix that.

What You Do	How You Do It
1. **Locate and select any instance of Burke Properties.**	a. To navigate to the top of the document, **press Page Up.**
	b. In the first sentence under "About Us", **select "Burke Properties" and the trailing space.**

About·Us¶
Burke·Properties·was

2. **Create an AutoText entry named *Burke Properties*.**

a. With "Burke Properties" selected, **choose Insert→AutoText→New.**

You may have to expand the Insert menu.

b. In the Please Name Your AutoText Entry text box, **leave Burke Properties as the default name for the new AutoText entry.**

c. **Click OK** to create the entry.

If prompted to redefine the AutoText entry, click Yes.

---

3. On page 3, **insert the "Burke Properties" AutoText entry before "Locations."**

a. To navigate to page 3, **press Page Down six times.**

b. **Place the insertion point before the "L" in "Locations."**

c. **Type *burk* and press Enter** to insert the Burke Properties AutoText entry.

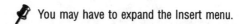

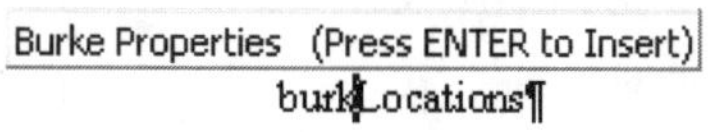

---

4. **How might you use AutoText on your job?**

TOPIC E

Move and Copy Text

There may be occasions when you want to move or reuse text—perhaps in the same document or in another document. With Word, you can do so quickly and easily. In this topic, you will explore ways to move and copy text.

If you want to re-purpose or rearrange blocks of text, copying and moving makes retyping unnecessary, thereby saving time as well as avoiding making typing mistakes. For instance, you are making changes to the annual report you wrote. Management wants to see how the report will look if you move around several of the sections. Additionally, they want you to include the new product information that's in this month's catalog insert. You could spend a lot of time retyping, or you could move and copy the text.

Clipboard Task Pane

The Clipboard task pane is a storage area that shows copied or cut items. As you cut and copy items from any open program, the items are collected on the Clipboard task pane. You can easily paste any item from the Clipboard in any order, regardless of the order in which the items were copied. (See Figure 2-3.)

Figure 2-3: *The Clipboard task pane.*

Clipboard Task Pane Tips

The Clipboard task pane can hold up to 24 items and is available in any Office System application. When you cut or copy the 25th item, without warning, the Clipboard task pane drops the oldest entry and adds the new one as the first item on the Click An Item To Paste list. The contents of the Clipboard task pane remain available until you exit all Office applications or exit Windows. Clicking Clear All in the task pane will also erase the items from the list. To open the Office Clipboard, choose Edit→Office Clipboard or press Ctrl+C twice. However, it appears automatically if you cut or copy two items, one after the other, without pasting.

How to Move and Copy Text

Procedure Reference: Move a Single Text Selection to a New Location

To move a single text selection:

1. Select the text you want to move.
2. Cut the selected text.
   - On the Standard toolbar, click the Cut button  .
   - Choose Edit→Cut.
   - Press Ctrl+X.
   - Or right-click to display a shortcut menu and choose Cut.
3. Place the insertion point where you want to move the text.
4. Paste the cut text.
   - On the Standard toolbar, click the Paste button  .
   - Choose Edit→Paste.
   - Press Ctrl+V.
   - Or right-click to display a shortcut menu and select Paste.

Drag and Drop

When you only need to move text a short distance, it may be quicker to drag it. To do this, simply select the text, press the mouse button, drag the text to where you want it to be, and release the mouse button to drop the selection in the new location. Note that dragging and dropping a selection does not add it to the Clipboard task pane.

Paste Options

When you paste an item, the Paste Options smart tag can be used to change how the pasted text is formatted. (See Table 2-6.)

Table 2-6: *Paste Options Explained*

Option	Description
Keep Source Formatting	Pastes the item as is, retaining the original formatting so the pasted item looks just like it did when it was copied.
Match Destination Formatting	The copied item's original formatting is replaced by the formatting used at the destination where item is pasted.
Keep Text Only	Pastes only the item, stripping all formatting that may have been copied.
Apply Style Or Formatting	Displays the Styles And Formatting task pane.

Procedure Reference: Move Several Text Selections to a New Location

To move several text selections:

1. Select the text you want to move.

2. Cut the selected text.
3. Repeat steps 1 and 2 to cut other text selections to the Clipboard task pane.
4. Place the insertion point where you want to move the text.
5. In the Clipboard task pane, click the cut item that you want to paste into the document.
6. Repeat steps 4 and 5 as needed.

Procedure Reference: Copy a Single Text Selection to a New Location

To copy a single text selection:

1. Select the text you want to copy.
2. Copy the selected text.
   - On the Standard toolbar, click the Copy button .
   - Choose Edit→Copy.
   - Press Ctrl+C.
   - Or right-click to display a shortcut menu and select Copy.
3. Place the insertion point where you want to paste the copied text.
4. Paste the copied text.

Procedure Reference: Copy Several Text Selections to a New Location

To copy several text selections:

1. Select the first text selection you want to copy.
2. Copy the selected text.
3. Repeat steps 1 and 2 to copy other text selections to the Clipboard task pane.
4. Place the insertion point where you want to paste the copied text.
5. In the Clipboard task pane, click the copied text item that you want to paste into the document.
6. Repeat steps 4 and 5 as needed.

Procedure Reference: Switch Between Open Documents

To switch between open documents:

You can also switch between documents by selecting the document's icon from the Windows taskbar.

1. Choose Window to display a file name list of open documents. The file name in the active window has a check mark next to it.
2. Select the document you want to display in the active window.

ACTIVITY 2-6

Moving Text within a Document

Setup:

My Second Draft is open.

Scenario:

As you were reviewing the draft document, you noticed some paragraphs that seem out of place. On page 1, you believe that the "Our Company Affiliations" heading and the paragraph that immediately follows it should be moved down in the document, so that they precede the paragraph on page 2 that begins with, "The Association of Realtors...." The other paragraph that seems misplaced is the short "Our Services" heading on page 2. It should be on page 1, just before the paragraph that begins with "Burke Properties relocation services...."

What You Do	How You Do It
1. From page 1, **cut the text from the "Our Company Affiliations" heading through the blank line after the "Burke Properties is a privately owned..." paragraph.**	a. Near the bottom of page 1, **select the following three paragraphs: "Our Company Affiliations," "Burke Properties is a privately owned...", and the subsequent blank line paragraph.**

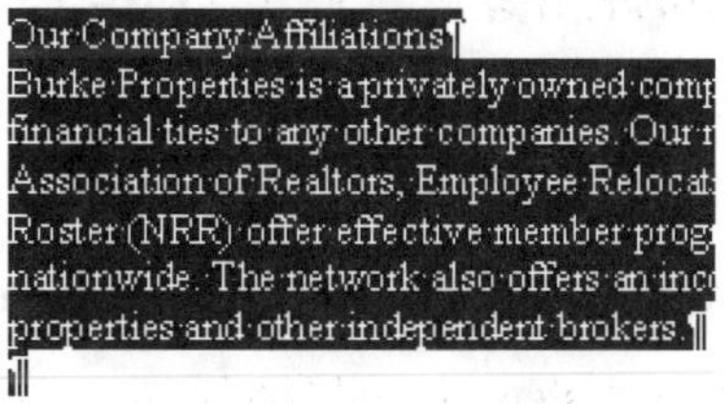

Our Company Affiliations¶
Burke Properties is a privately owned comp
financial ties to any other companies. Our r
Association of Realtors, Employee Relocat
Roster (NRR) offer effective member prog
nationwide. The network also offers an inc
properties and other independent brokers.¶
¶

b. On the Standard toolbar, **click the Cut button** .

You may need to display the Standard toolbar's Toolbar Options button to see the Cut button.

2. **Move the cut text to page 2, just before the "The Association of Realtors..." paragraph.**

   a. On page 2, **place the insertion point before the "T" in "The Association of Realtors..." paragraph.**

   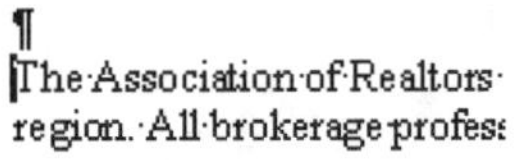
   ¶
   The·Association·of·Realtors·
   region.·All·brokerage·profes

   b. On the Standard toolbar, **click the Paste button** .

---

3. From page 2, **move the "Our Services" paragraph to page 1, just before the "Burke Properties services..." paragraph.**

   a. On page 2, **select the "Our Services" paragraph.**

   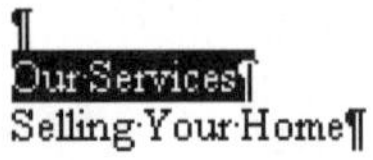
   ¶
   Our·Services¶
   Selling·Your·Home¶

   b. **Cut the selected text.**

   The Clipboard task pane may be displayed, showing the last two items you cut from the document.

   c. On page 1, **place the insertion point before the "B" in the "Burke Properties services..." paragraph.**

   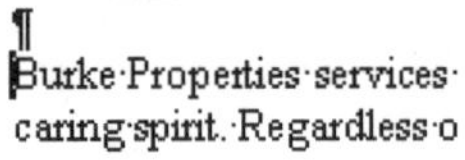
   ¶
   Burke·Properties·services·
   caring·spirit.·Regardless·o

   d. **Paste the cut text.** (Click the Paste button on the Standard toolbar.)

ACTIVITY 2-7

Copying Text Between Documents

Data Files:

- Nolan Letter.doc

Setup:

My Second Draft is open.

Scenario:

You realize that some content is missing from the draft document, specifically a list of things a realtor does for his or her clients under the "Selling Your Home" paragraph on page 2, and the Burke Properties guarantee on page 3 below the "Our Guarantee" paragraph. Fortunately, you recall seeing that information in a letter written to Beth Nolan.

What You Do	How You Do It
1. In Nolan Letter, **display the Clipboard task pane and copy the "Here's what a realtor..." heading and list and the "We are so sure..." sentence.**	a. From the My Documents folder, **open Nolan Letter.**
	b. To display the Clipboard task pane, **choose Edit→Office Clipboard.**
	c. In the letter, **select the "Here's what a realtor..." list.**

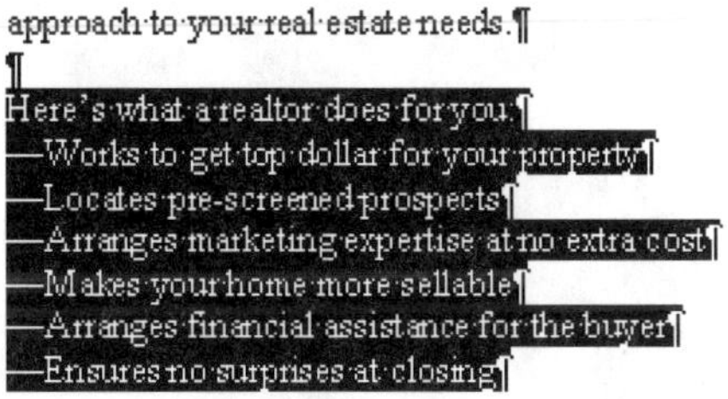
approach·to·your·real·estate·needs.¶
¶
Here's·what·a·realtor·does·for·you:¶
—Works·to·get·top·dollar·for·your·property¶
—Locates·pre-screened·prospects¶
—Arranges·marketing·expertise·at·no·extra·cost¶
—Makes·your·home·more·sellable¶
—Arranges·financial·assistance·for·the·buyer¶
—Ensures·no·surprises·at·closing¶

d. On the Standard toolbar, **click the Copy button** to copy the selection.

Notice that the selection has been copied to the beginning of the Clipboard task pane.

e. At the bottom of the letter, after the PS, **select the sentence "We are so sure...", including the paragraph mark.**

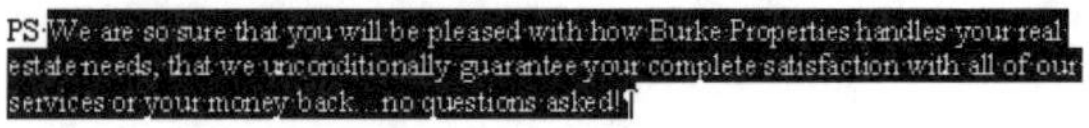

f. **Copy the selection** to add it to the Clipboard task pane.

---

2. Back in the draft document, just after the "Selling Your Home" paragraph on page 2, **use the Clipboard task pane to paste a copy of the "Here's what a realtor..." item.**

a. **Choose Window→1 My Second Draft.**

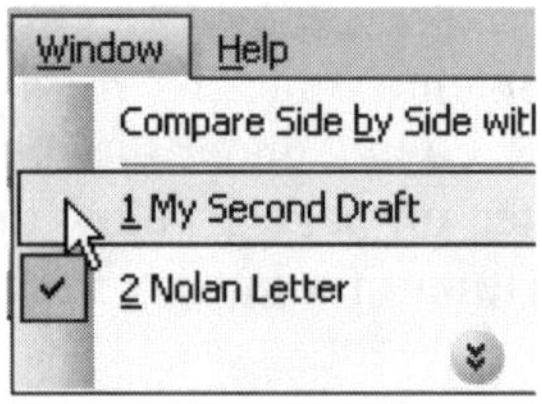

⚠ If necessary, redisplay the Clipboard task pane.

b. In the My Second Draft document, on the second page, **place the insertion point on the blank line below "Selling Your Home" paragraph.**

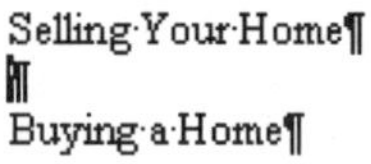

c. In the Clipboard task pane's Click An Item To Paste list box, **click once on the "Here's what a realtor..." item** to paste a copy of it into the document.

---

3. On page 3, just below the "Our Guarantee" paragraph, **paste a copy of the "We are so sure..." item.**

   a. On page 3, **place the insertion point on the blank line below the "Our Guarantee" paragraph.**

   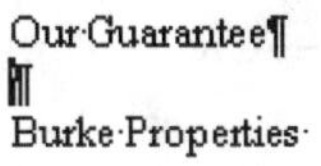
   Our·Guarantee¶
   ¶
   Burke·Properties·

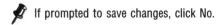

   b. In the Clipboard task pane's Click An Item To Paste list box, **click once on the "We are so sure..." item** to paste a copy of it into the document.

---

4. **Close the Nolan letter.**

   a. **Switch back to the Nolan Letter window.**

   b. **Choose File→Close** to close the document.

   If prompted to save changes, click No.

TOPIC F

Delete Blocks of Text

As you edit a document you may have some text that is no longer necessary. You will want to delete that text so it doesn't clutter your document. In this topic, you will delete blocks of extra text.

Removing text is a useful way to make your document's message as clear and as concise as possible. Some text deletions may be small, which can easily be handled by pressing the Backspace key a few times. But imagine deleting several paragraphs or pages in a document using the Backspace key. You would have to press Backspace repeatedly—perhaps hundreds or thousands of times! There's a big risk of deleting too much text, as the insertion point charges back though your text. Fortunately, in Word you can remove text selections in a more efficient and controlled way.

How to Delete Text

Procedure Reference: Delete Text

To delete blocks of text:

1. Select the text you want to delete.

   Be sure to select any punctuation, spaces, or paragraph marks if desired.

2. Delete the text.
   - Press Delete.
   - Press Backspace.
   - Or choose Edit→Clear→Contents.

ACTIVITY 2-8

Deleting Blocks of Text

Setup:

My Second Draft is open with the Clipboard task pane displayed.

Scenario:

This document is supposed to be a general introduction to Burke Properties and its offerings. Some of the content is too specific and should be deleted.

What You Do	How You Do It
1. On page 1, **delete the text from "Relocation Team:" through the blank line just above "Our Company Affiliations."**	a. Near the bottom of page 1, **place the insertion point before the "R" in "Relocation Team."**

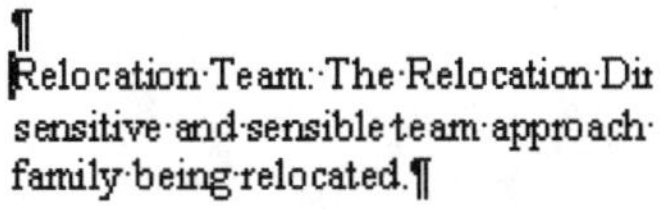
¶
Relocation·Team:·The·Relocation·Di
sensitive·and·sensible·team·approach·
family·being·relocated.¶

b. To display the "Our Company Affiliations" paragraph on page 2, in the vertical scroll bar, **click below the scroll box.**

c. To extend the selection, **press and hold Shift, then click the mouse pointer before the "O" in "Our Company Affiliations."**

d. **Release Shift** to select the block of text.

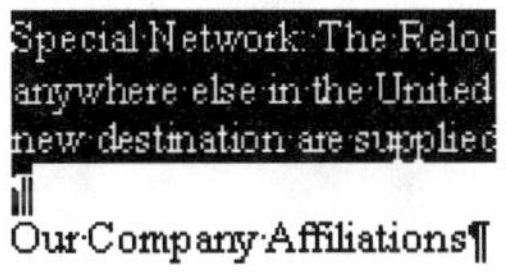
Special·Network:·The·Relo
anywhere·else·in·the·United
new·destination·are·supplie
Our·Company·Affiliations¶

e. **Press Delete.**

2. **Is the deleted text added to the Clipboard task pane?**___

What You Do	How You Do It
3. On page 2, **delete the text from "Mortgage rates for..." through the blank line just above "Currently, with mortgage rates...."**	a. On page 2, just below the "Buying a Home" heading, **place the insertion point before the "M" in "Mortgage rates for..."**

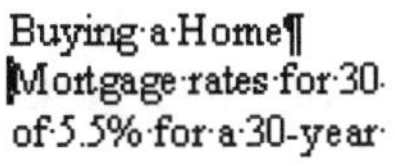
Buying·a·Home¶
Mortgage·rates·for·30·
of·5.5%·for·a·30-year·

b. **Select all of the text up to "Currently, with mortgage rates...."**

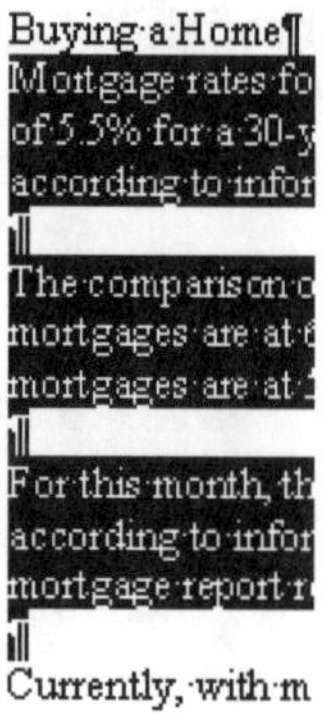

c. **Press Delete.**

4. **After deleting the text block, can you paste it somewhere else?___**

TOPIC G

Undo Changes

As you enter or edit text, you may make mistakes or simply realize that you liked something the way it was before you made changes. In this topic, you will reverse changes that you make.

You've just finished writing a long letter to your manager, outlining why you should get a raise. It had details of all the projects you worked on this year and you decide to go get some coffee before you bring it to your performance review. While you were gone, a co-worker decides to play a practical joke on you by deleting all the text from the document. Of course, you neglected to save the document before you went for coffee. Is everything lost? No. Although everything appears to be gone, it really isn't. Word provides you with a safety net, enabling you to undo changes made to an open document.

How to Undo Changes

Procedure Reference: Undo a Single Change

To undo a single change made in an open document:

1. Perform an action.
2. Undo the action.
    - On the Standard toolbar, click the Undo button  .
    - Choose Edit→Undo.

- Or, press Ctrl+Z.

Procedure Reference: Undo Several Changes

To undo several changes made in an open document:

1. Perform several actions.
2. On the Standard toolbar, display the Undo drop-down list.
3. Select the number of changes to be undone.

Procedure Reference: Redo a Single Change

To redo a single change made in an open document:

1. Undo an action.
2. Redo the undone action.
   - On the Standard toolbar, click the Redo button  .
   - Or, press Ctrl+Y.

Procedure Reference: Redo Several Changes

To redo a change made in an open document:

1. Undo several actions.
2. On the Standard toolbar, display the Redo drop-down list.
3. Select the number of changes to be redone.

Undo/Redo a Series of Changes

You can undo or redo a series of actions in the opposite order that the changes were originally performed. This is done using the drop-down lists available on both the Undo or Redo buttons. Simply display the list and select the number of changes you want to undo or redo. (Figure 2-4 shows how to Undo a series of actions.) You cannot pick a specific change from the list without undoing or redoing all previous changes. Also, Undo and Redo work only for the current working session. Once you close a document, the Undo and Redo lists are cleared.

⚠ While you can undo or redo most actions, certain actions, such as opening, saving, or printing a document, cannot be undone.

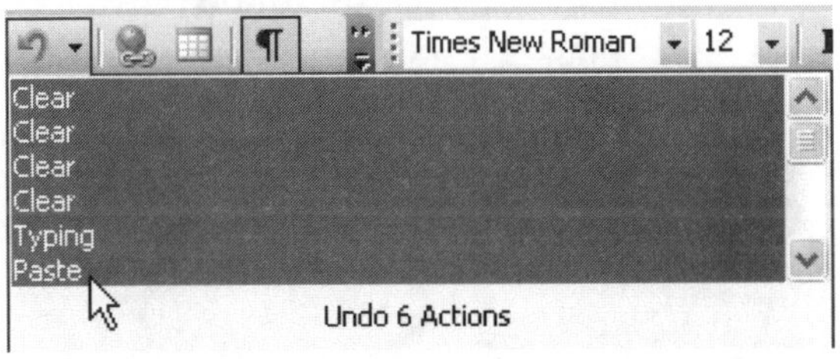

Figure 2-4: ***Undoing a series of actions.***

Delete, Cut, and Clear

Unlike items you cut, deleted items cannot be pasted because they are not collected by the Clipboard task pane. The deleted item can be restored only by using the Undo command. Additionally, when you press Delete you are not technically deleting the selection. Word refers to deleting as clearing. It's a subtle distinction, but one worth knowing.

ACTIVITY 2-9

Recovering Deleted Blocks of Text

Setup:

My Second Draft is open.

Scenario:

You heard that the Kentucky, Ohio, and Texas offices were going to be closed soon so you decide to delete those items from the Burke Properties Locations list. After a while, you find out that what you heard about the Texas offices was only a rumor. And there's a possibility that the Kentucky and Ohio offices may remain open too. You decide to restore those three blocks of text to the list of offices at the end of the document.

What You Do	How You Do It
1. **Delete the Kentucky, Ohio, and Texas blocks of text, as well as the blank lines after each.**	a. **Select and delete Kentucky, including Lexington and the blank line that follows.**
	b. **Select and delete Ohio, including Cleveland, Toledo, and the blank line that follows.**
	c. **Select and delete Texas, including Dallas and San Antonio.**
2. **Undo the Texas text block deletion.**	a. To restore the Texas, Dallas, and San Antonio block of text, on the Standard toolbar, **click the Undo button**  **once.**
3. **Undo the Ohio and Kentucky deletions at the same time.**	a. **Display the Undo button's drop-down list.** 

b. **Move the mouse pointer down over the second Clear action so that both are highlighted.**

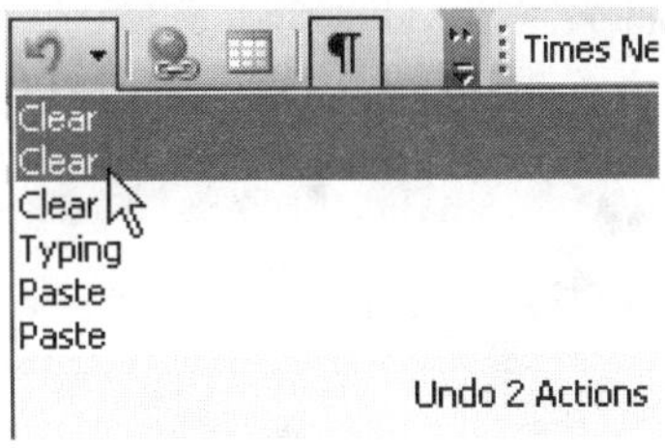

c. To restore both the Ohio and the Kentucky text blocks at the same time, **click the second Clear action.**

---

4. The Planning Department has confirmed that the Kentucky offices are indeed closing. **Redo the Kentucky text block deletion.**

a. To delete the Kentucky text block again, on the Standard toolbar, **click the Redo Clear button**  **once.**

TOPIC H

Find and Replace Text

Now that you have performed some basic editing tasks, you can see that scrolling through a document to locate and fix errors is very time-consuming. There's a better way to perform these types of edits. In this topic, you will quickly and efficiently search for and replace text.

If you're working on a short document, it's not too difficult to find the text you're looking for if you just scroll up and down. However, if you're looking for a client's name in a 200-page legal document, that method is like looking for a needle in a haystack. How are you going to locate every occurrence of a client's name? And what if your client changes her last name from Smith to Tompkin? How are you going to change each occurrence of Smith to Tompkin? Scrolling is no longer an efficient option. That could take hours and you may miss one or two occurrences of the name. Word enables you to locate every occurrence of the text you want to find, then presents you with the opportunity to selectively replace an occurrence or replace them all with the click of a button.

Find and Replace Options

Find and Replace options can help you quickly locate just what you are looking for in a document. (See Figure 2-5.)

- Search Options can be used to search the document in a specific direction or to locate specific text patterns.
- The Format button can be use to locate specific instances of formatting.

- The Special button can be used to enter codes for non-printing characters in the Find What and Replace With text boxes.

When the More button is clicked, it changes to the Less button.

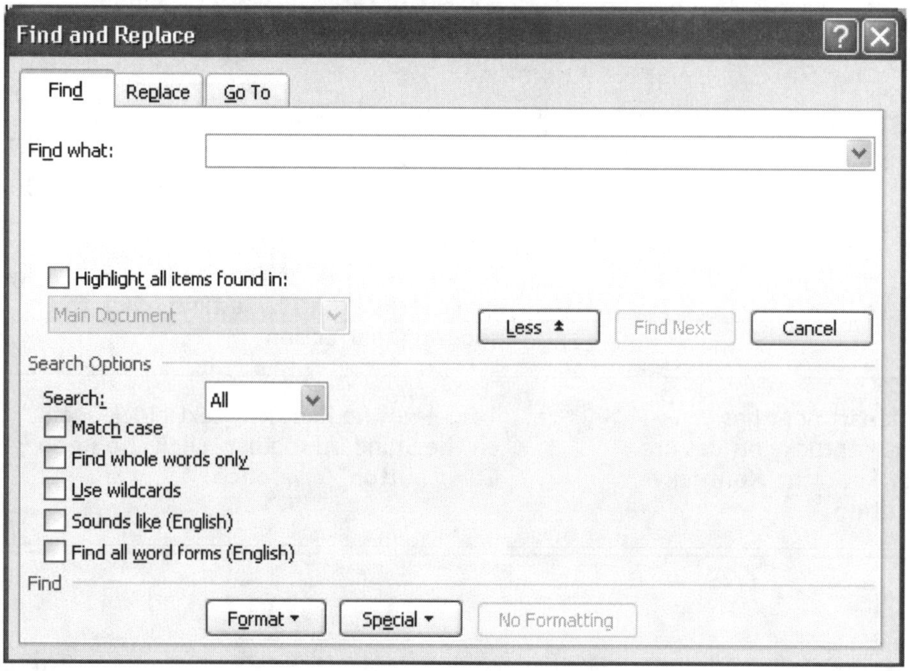

Figure 2-5: *Search Options displayed in the Find And Replace dialog box.*

How to Find and Replace Text

Procedure Reference: Find Text

To find text in your document:

1. Display the Find tab in the Find And Replace dialog box.
   - Choose Edit→Find.
   - Or press Ctrl+F.
2. In the Find What text box, type the text you want to locate.
3. If necessary, set search options.
   a. Click the More button to display search options.
   b. Set the desired option(s).
   c. Click the Less button to hide the search options.
4. Click Find Next to locate the first occurrence of the text in the document. Continue clicking Find Next to advance to the next occurrence.
5. When Word has finished searching the document, click OK.
6. When finished, click Cancel to close the Find And Replace dialog box.

Highlight All Items Found

You can use the Find command to highlight all instances of a found item in a document. On the Find tab in the Find And Replace dialog box, type the text you want to locate in the Find What text box, select the Highlight All Items Found In option, and click Find All. Every instance of the text will be highlighted in the document. The number of found items is also displayed in the Find And Replace dialog box.

Procedure Reference: Replace Text in Your Document

To search for and replace text in your document:

1. Display the Replace tab in the Find And Replace dialog box.
   - Choose Edit→Replace.
   - Or press Ctrl+H.
2. In the Find What text box, type the text you want to locate.
3. If necessary, set search options.
4. In the Replace With text box, type the text that you want to substitute for any found occurrences.

   Include any special characters, such as tabs, double-spaces, and the like.

5. Click Find Next to begin the search. In the document's text area, Word will highlight the first occurrence of the found text. You can then make one of these decisions:
   - Click Replace to replace the highlighted text and continue searching for the next occurrence. In this way, you replace selected text on a case-by-case basis.
   - Click Find Next to leave the highlighted text unchanged and continue searching for the next occurrence.
   - Click Replace All to replace all occurrences of the text at the same time. Be careful—if you use Replace All, you can easily make changes you didn't intend to make.

     If you change your mind about a replace operation, click the Undo button on the Standard toolbar. If you used the Replace button, Word will undo the replacements one by one. If you used the Replace All button, Word will undo all of the replacements at once.

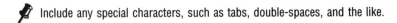

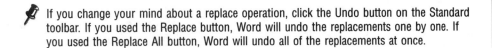

ACTIVITY 2-10

Finding and Replacing Text

Setup:

My Second Draft is open. If necessary, close the Clipboard task pane.

Scenario:

The last time a document like this was reviewed, Burke Properties wasn't properly capitalized in all cases. The "B" in Burke and the "P" in Properties should always be capitalized. Also, as part of a new Human Resource department initiative, many job titles have been updated. You have been asked to make sure that wherever you find the job title "broker" that it is changed to "agent."

What You Do	How You Do It
1. **Prepare to search the document for any lowercase instances of "burke properties."**	a. **Move the insertion point to the top of the document.**
	b. **Choose Edit→Replace** to display the Replace tab in the Find And Replace dialog box. You may need to expand the Edit menu to display the Replace option.
	c. In the Find What text box, **type *burke properties*** with the "b" and "p" lowercase.
	d. **Click the More button** to display the search options.
	e. Under Search Options, **check the Match Case check box.** When you check the Match Case check box, it is listed below the Find What text box.
	f. **Click Less** to reduce the size of the dialog box.

2. **Replace "burke properties" with "Burke Properties."**

a. In the Replace With text box, **type *Burke Properties*** with a capital "B" and a capital "P."

b. **Click Find Next** to find the first occurrence of "burke properties."

You can move the Find And Replace dialog box out of the way to see the found text in the document.

c. **Click Replace** to replace the lowercase instance with the uppercase version.

d. **Click Replace** to replace the next instance.

e. When Word has finished searching the document, **click OK.**

---

3. **Prepare to replace instances of the "broker" job title with "agent." This time, don't use the Match Case search option.**

a. In the Find What text box, **type *broker***

b. **Press Tab** to move the insertion point into the Replace With text box.

c. **Type *agent***

d. **Click More.**

e. **Uncheck the Match Case check box.**

Notice the option is removed from below the Find What text box.

f. **Click Less.**

---

4. **Find and replace instances of the word "broker" with the word "agent."**

a. **Click Find Next** to find the first occurrence of "broker."

b. In the text area, **observe the selected text.**

·real·estate·brokerage·

c. **Click Find Next** to ignore that occurrence and to continue the search.

d. **Click Replace** to replace "broker" with "agent" and continue the search.

e. In the next occurrence, The "broker" part of the word "brokers" is selected. Since replacing "broker" with "agent" in this case would work, **click Replace.**

f. When appropriate, **continue replacing any remaining occurrences of "broker" with "agent."**

g. When finished, **click OK and close the Find And Replace dialog box.**

---

5. **Save your changes to My Second Draft and close the file.**

a. To update the file with the changes you have made, on the Standard toolbar, **click the Save button** .

b. **Choose File→Close.**

Lesson 2 Follow-up

In this lesson, you learned how to navigate in a document other than just scrolling. You made minor edits by inserting text for clarification as well as more comprehensive edits by selecting and deleting large blocks of text to conserve space in your document. You created an AutoText entry to insert text more quickly and more accurately than if you were to type the entry's full text each time. You reused some text by moving and copying it within a document and between documents. You reversed changes you made using the Undo command. You also located and replaced text as needed. In the next lesson, you will learn some useful ways to format text so it stands out in your documents.

1. **How do you currently edit documents?**

2. **Compared to how you currently edit your documents, how can the editing techniques presented in this lesson help you work more efficiently?**

Notes

LESSON 3
Formatting Text

Lesson Time
1 hour(s)

Lesson Objectives:

In this lesson, you will format text.

You will:

- Change the font and font size of selected text.
- Apply font styles and effects to selected text.
- Change text color.
- Highlight text.
- Copy formatting from one text selection to another.
- Clear formatting from formatted text.
- Find and replace text formatting.

Introduction

Now that you can enter and edit text in a document, it's a good time to make your text more visually appealing. Whether to make a selection stand out from surrounding text or to meet a stylistic requirement, formatting text can enhance your document. In this lesson, you will learn some ways to format text to do just that.

There will be times when you want a word, phrase, or line of text to stand out from your document's main text. With a variety of font colors, sizes, and styles, you can direct your reader's attention to important information by formatting characters.

TOPIC A

Change Font and Size

You have a document with text that all looks the same. The document's message could benefit from making some of the text more distinctive. In this topic, you will change the font and size of selected text to distinguish it from surrounding text.

The primary goal of any document is to get someone to read it. The font choices you make can help you achieve that goal. On the one hand, subtle but intentional changes to the font and font size can make your text more professional and readable. By varying the font's size, you can divide your document into more accessible and memorable pieces for the reader. By varying the font you use, you can draw attention to critical concepts. On the other hand, if you use too many fonts, or vary the font sizes without a good reason, you can make it virtually impossible for anyone to read your document without experiencing a headache.

Fonts

A *font* is a named set of characters that combines several design qualities. The set of characters includes letters, numbers, punctuation marks, and so on.

Figure 3-1 shows an example of two common fonts.

Arial:	Times New Roman:
Aa, Bb, Cc, Dd	Aa, Bb, Cc, Dd
1, 2, 3, 4	1, 2, 3, 4
! @ # $	! @ # $

Figure 3-1: *Each font includes several qualities.*

Font Size Measurement

Font size refers specifically to a font's height. The size is measured in points, sometimes abbreviated as pt or pts. Each point is about 1/72 of an inch. So if text has a 72-pt font size, it is about an inch tall. Word's default font size is 12 pt.

Shopping through fonts -
format > font
can 'down arrow' through list

18 points

36 points

72 points = 1 inch

Figure 3-2: *Font size measurements.*

How to Change the Font and Font Size

Procedure Reference: Change the Font

To change the font and font size of text:

1. Select the text you want to affect.
2. Change the font.
   - Using the Font drop-down list box on the Formatting toolbar, display the Font drop-down list box Times New Roman ▾ , and select the desired font.

     Press Ctrl+Shift+F to select the Font drop-down list box.

   - Or, using the Font Dialog Box, choose Format→Font. From the Font list, select the desired size. Click OK.

Procedure Reference: Change the Font Size

To change the font size of text:

1. Select the text you want to affect.
2. Change the font size.
   - Using the Font Size drop-down list box on the Formatting toolbar, display the Font Size drop-down list box 12 ▾ , and select the desired font size.

     Press Ctrl+Shift+P to select the Font Size drop-down list box.

   - Or, using the Font Dialog Box, choose Format→Font. From the Size list, select the desired size. Click OK.

     Press Ctrl+D to display the Font dialog box.

ACTIVITY 3-1

Changing the Font and Font Sizes

Data Files:

- Relocation Services.doc

Scenario:

All of the text in the Relocation Services document looks the same, so the content seems to blend together. You decide that changing the font and font sizes for some of the text would divide the document into more readable and memorable paragraphs.

What You Do	How You Do It
1. In Relocation Services, **make the paragraph "Our Relocation Services" Arial.**	a. **Open Relocation Services.**
	b. **Select the text "Our Relocation Services."**
	c. On the Formatting toolbar, **click the Font button's drop-down list arrow** to display the Font drop-down list box.

d. From the top of the Font drop-down list box, **select Arial.**

Arial is at the top of the Font drop-down list box because it has been used recently.

2. **Change the font size of the selected text to 24 points.**

a. With the text still selected, on the Formatting toolbar, **click the Font Size button's drop-down list arrow** to display the Font Size drop-down list box .

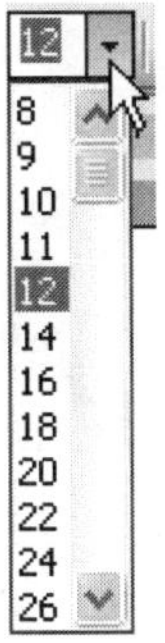

b. From the Font Size drop-down list box, **select 24.**

---

3. **Select the remaining two headings and change the font to Arial 24 point.**

a. **Select "Our Relocation Staff."**

b. To add to the selection, while pointing in the selection bar to the left of the text "Our Relocation Fees," **press and hold Ctrl and click the mouse button once.**

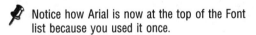

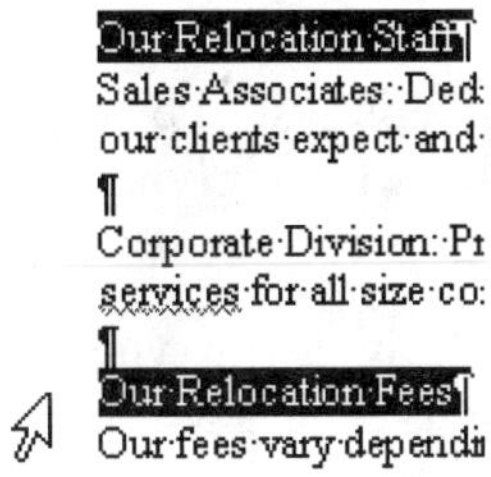

c. From the Font drop-down list box, **select Arial.**

Notice how Arial is now at the top of the Font list because you used it once.

d. From the Font Size drop-down list box, **select 24.**

e. **Deselect the text.**

---

4. **Change the font of "Relocation Network:" to Arial 11 pt.**
   a. **Select "Relocation Network:"**
   b. From the Font drop-down list box, **select Arial.**
   c. From the Font Size drop-down list box, **select 11.**
   d. **Deselect the text.**

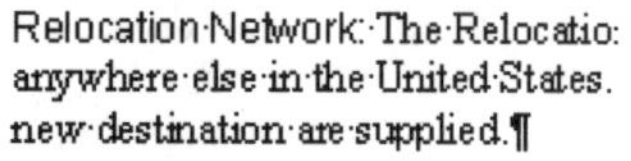

Relocation·Network:·The·Relocatio:
anywhere·else·in·the·United·States.
new·destination·are·supplied.¶

5. **Save the document as *My Relocation Services*.**

TOPIC B

Apply Font Styles and Effects

Changing text's font and size is just one way to draw attention to selected text. You can further enhance how a font looks by applying different font styles and effects. That's what you will do in this topic.

As you drive on an interstate highway, your attention often begins to wander. But when you see a road sign, it helps focus your attention by displaying useful information. Font styles and effects offer a benefit similar to road signs. By applying such formatting to your critical snippets of text, you can easily guide the readers' eyes and keep them focused on your message. The fact that font styles and effects both can make your documents more professional looking is an added benefit.

Font Styles and Effects

Font styles and effects are ways to enhance the appearance of typed characters. The bold font style, for instance, can help a reader to locate important text, while the subscript effect may be used to type formulas or equations. Figure 3-3 shows some common examples of each type of character formatting.

Font Styles:	Effects:
Regular	~~Strikethrough~~
Bold	Superscript and Subscript
Italic	Shadow
Bold Italic	Outline
	SMALL CAPS

Figure 3-3: *Examples of font styles and effects.*

How to Apply Font Styles and Effects

Procedure Reference: Apply Font Styles

To apply font styles:

1. Select the text you want to affect.
2. Apply the desired font styles.
   - On the Formatting toolbar, click the Bold **B**, Italic *I*, or Underline U buttons .

     These buttons are toggles. Click them once to apply the formatting. Click them again to remove the formatting.

   - In the Font dialog box, under Font Style, select the desired font style from the list. (To apply an underline, make a selection from the Underline Style drop-down list box.)
   - Or, press the corresponding shortcut key: Ctrl+B for bold, Ctrl+I for italic, or Ctrl+U for underline.

Procedure Reference: Apply Effects Using the Font Dialog Box

To apply effects:

1. Select the text you want to affect.
2. Display the Font dialog box. (Choose Format→Font.)
3. Select the desired effects.
4. Click OK to close the Font dialog box and apply the effects to your text.

Procedure Reference: Repeat the Last Action

To repeat an action:

1. Perform an action.
2. Repeat the action.
   - Choose Edit→Repeat.
   - Press F4.
   - Or, press Ctrl+Y.

Some actions cannot be repeated, such as saving or opening a document.

Repeat Versus Redo

After you perform an action, such as typing text, you can quickly repeat the action without performing the same steps again. Just choose Edit→Repeat *Action Name*. (The name of the last action you performed is appended to the Edit→Repeat menu option. For instance, if you want to repeat typing, the menu option is Edit→Repeat Typing.) Redo only works after using the Undo tool.

ACTIVITY 3-2

Applying Font Styles and Effects

Setup:

My Relocation Services is open.

Scenario:

With the new font and font size applied to the "Relocation Network" inline heading, it looks a little different, but it could benefit from more character formatting to make it standout further. You decide that applying font styles and effects would accomplish that.

What You Do	How You Do It
1. **Make "Relocation Network:" bold.**	a. **Select "Relocation Network:"**
	b. On the Formatting toolbar, **click the Bold button** B to apply the bold font style.

2. **Apply a double underline and the Small Caps effect to "Relocation Network:"**

a. With "Relocation Network:" still selected, **choose Format→Font.**

Notice that the font, font style, and size settings match those of the selected text.

b. From the Underline Style drop-down list box, **select the fourth option, Double Underline.**

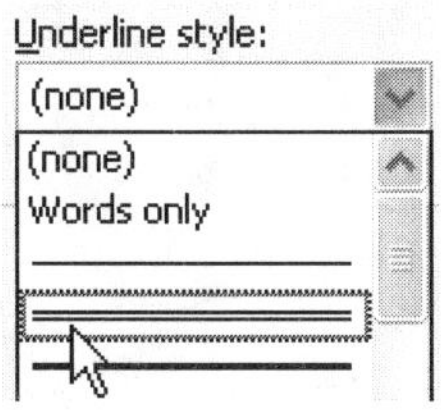

c. In the Effects area of the dialog box, **check the Small Caps check box.**

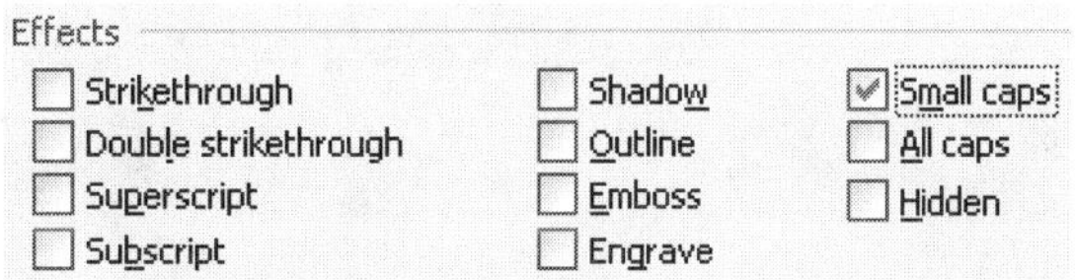

The Preview area displays the selected effect.

d. **Click OK** to apply the formatting.

e. **Deselect the text.**

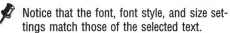

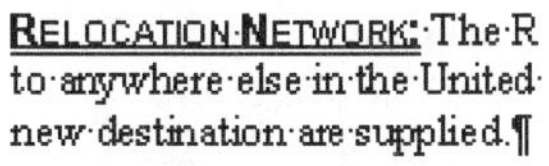

3. **Italicize the publication title, "Your Relocation Checklist."**

   a. **Near the top of the document, select "Your Relocation Checklist."**

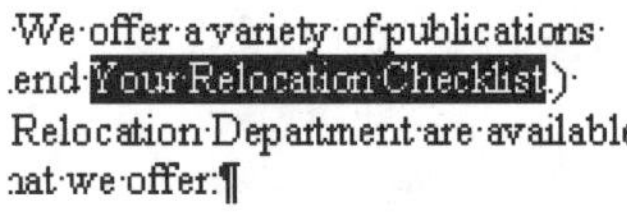
We·offer·a·variety·of·publications·
.end·Your·Relocation·Checklist.)·
Relocation·Department·are·available·
ıat·we·offer:¶

   b. **To apply the italic font style to the selected text, on the Formatting toolbar, click the Italic button.**

4. **Repeat the italic font style for "unconditionally guarantee" in the last paragraph.**

   When you use the Repeat function, you must apply it immediately following the action you want to repeat.

   a. **Scroll to the bottom of the document and select "unconditionally guarantee."**

   b. **Choose Edit→Repeat Italic.**

   You may have to expand the Edit menu.

   c. **Deselect the text.**

TOPIC C

Change Text Color

Font styles and effects draw attention to words and phrases. Adding color to your text is another effective method for making text stand out. In this topic, you will change text color.

If you saw a flamingo in the polar bear exhibit at the zoo, the flamingo's bright colors would clearly stand out against the snow white background. Similarly, when you add color to a document, it too stands out against the paper's white background. Though most business documents are still printed in black and white, with the growing availability of color printers, adding color to your documents is becoming more and more common. Applying color sparingly to text is a powerful way to make that text stand apart, adding visual interest while pointing out significant information to the reader.

How to Change the Color of Text

Procedure Reference: Change Text Color

To change text color:

1. Select the text you want to affect.
2. Change the text color.

- On the Formatting toolbar, click the Font Color button's drop-down arrow  to display the color palette and select the desired color.
- Or, in the Font dialog box, from the Font Color drop-down list box, select the desired color, and click OK.

You can display colors other than those on the Color palette by selecting the More Colors option.

ACTIVITY 3-3

Changing Text Color

Setup:

My Relocation Services is open.

Scenario:

My Relocation Services is going to be printed on a color printer, so you can enhance the primary headings by changing their font colors. Also, to play up the fact that the guarantee promises that the client's money will be returned, you want to change the color of the words "money back" to reflect this.

What You Do	How You Do It
1. **Make "Our Relocation Services" dark blue.**	a. At the top of the document, **select "Our Relocation Services."**
	b. On the Formatting toolbar, **click the Font Color button's drop-down arrow** to display the color palette.

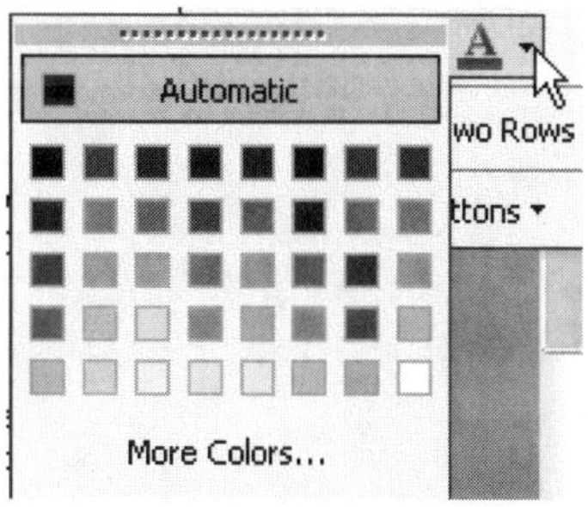

c. **Select Dark Blue.**

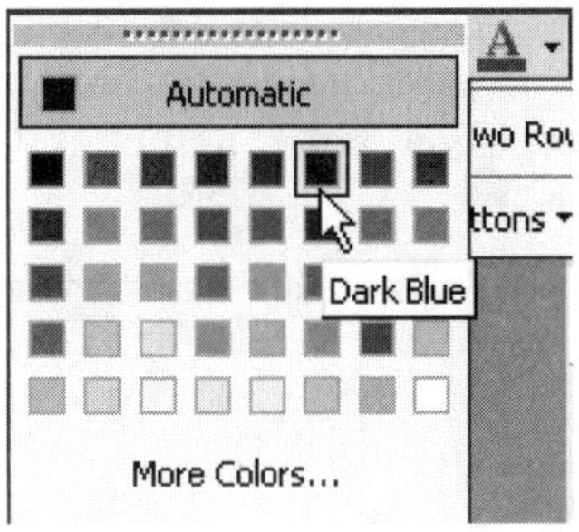

d. **Deselect the text.**

---

2. **Repeat the font color for "Our Relocation Staff" and "Our Relocation Fees."**

a. **Select "Our Relocation Staff."**

b. **Press and hold Ctrl while selecting "Our Relocation Fees"** to add the text to the selection.

c. **Choose Edit→Repeat Font Color.**

d. **Deselect the text.**

---

3. **Make "money back" green.**

a. In the last paragraph, **select "money back."**

b. From the Font Color button's color palette, **select Green.**

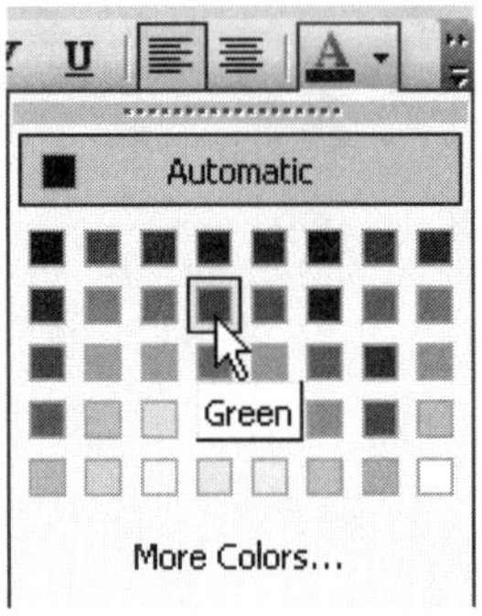

c. **Deselect the text.**

TOPIC D

Highlight Text

Changing fonts and applying font styles are effective to a point. But if you really want a word or sentence to jump off the page, nothing beats highlighting the text. In this topic, you will highlight text.

Most of us have used a pen-like highlighter to mark significant information as we read paper documents. Why? Because the bright color makes it easy to locate the key points that may be worth referring to again. The same idea holds true in Word. By highlighting key words, phrases, or sentences, you make it easier for the reader to locate important concepts or phrases by just glancing at the document on screen or on paper when the document is printed with a color printer.

How to Highlight Text

Procedure Reference: Apply Highlighting

To highlight text:

1. Select the text you want to affect.
2. Apply a highlight color.
    - To apply the default color, click the Highlight button  on the Formatting toolbar.
    - Or, to apply a different color, click the Highlight button's drop-down arrow and select the desired color from the color palette.

Highlighter Tips

Several things to keep in mind when highlighting text:

- The highlighter's default color is yellow. However, you can select other colors from the Highlight button's drop-down list box.
- Next, you can determine which color the highlighter is currently using by either looking at the Highlight button's icon or by placing the mouse pointer over the button. The ScreenTip shows the current color in parentheses.
- Lastly, highlighting works best for on-screen use or when the document is printed with a color printer. So if you plan to print to a black and white printer, use a light color or gray so the highlighted text can still be read.

Turn the Highlighter On and Off

You can turn on the highlighter by clicking the Highlight button on the Formatting toolbar. The mouse pointer changes to an I-beam with a highlighter  . You can then select the desired text to apply the default yellow highlight. The highlighter remains active until you turn it off by clicking the Highlight button again.

Procedure Reference: Remove Highlighting

To remove highlighting:

1. Select the highlighted text.

2. Click the Highlight button's drop-down arrow.
3. Select None.

ACTIVITY 3-4

Highlighting Text in a Document

Setup:

My Relocation Services is open.

Scenario:

Changing the font color of the text "money back" doesn't stand out like you thought it would. To really draw attention to it, you decide to use the highlighter. You also want your manager to review the percentages under Our Relocation Fees so you need them to stand out. Once the figures have been reviewed, they no longer need to stand out.

What You Do	How You Do It
1. **Highlight "money back."**	a. **Select the words "money back."**
You may need to use the Formatting toolbar's Toolbar Options button to locate the Highlight button.	b. On the Formatting toolbar, **click the Highlight button** to apply a yellow highlight to the text.

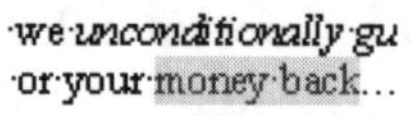

What You Do	How You Do It
2. **Highlight "5%-10%" in red.**	a. In the paragraph directly below Our Relocation Fees, **select the percentages "5%-10%."**
	b. **Display the Highlight button's drop-down list box.**
	c. **Select Red.**

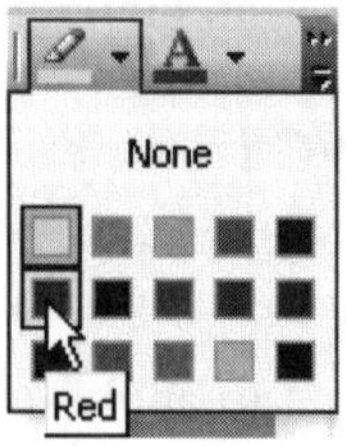

3. Your manager walks in and sees the percentages highlighted in red. She says they are correct. **Remove the highlight from the percentages.**

   a. **Select "5%-10%" again.**

   b. **Click the Highlight button's drop-down arrow.**

   c. **Select None** to remove the highlighting.

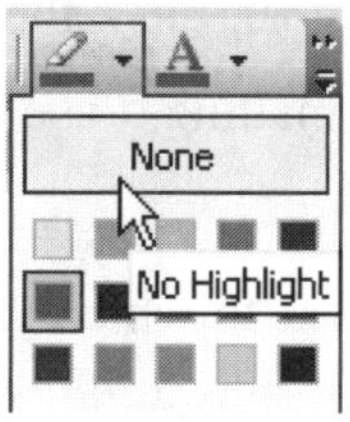

4. **Highlight "we unconditionally guarantee your complete satisfaction with all of our services or your money back...no questions asked!" in yellow.**

   a. **Select "we unconditionally guarantee your complete satisfaction with all of our services or your money back...no questions asked!"**

   b. **Click the Highlight button's drop-down arrow.**

   c. **Select Yellow.**

TOPIC E

Copy Formats

You have already copied and pasted text. Similarly, you can copy text formatting from one text selection to another. You will use the Format Painter tool to do that in this topic.

You just spent 10 minutes formatting the heading for an important report so that it looks exactly the way you want it to. Now, you need to format six other headings in the report exactly the same way. You could select each of the remaining headings and apply all the individual format options again, but that would take valuable time that you would rather use to edit the report. A better way would be to copy the formatting you just created and paste that formatting over the rest of the headings. That way you could save almost an hour and be assured that the headings are all formatted consistently.

Format Painter

The *Format Painter* is a tool  on the Standard toolbar, and it is used to copy a text selection's character or paragraph formatting to a new text selection. The Format Painter lets you duplicate formatting without duplicating effort.

How to Copy Text Formatting

Procedure Reference: Copy Text Formatting to a Text Selection

To copy text formatting and apply it to another text selection:

1. Select the text with the formatting you want to copy.
2. On the Standard toolbar, click the Format Painter button once. This copies the existing text formatting. (The mouse pointer changes to a paintbrush with an I-beam .)
3. Drag to select the text to which you want to apply the copied text formatting. The Format Painter immediately applies the copied formatting to the new selection.

You can also press Ctrl+Shift+C to copy a selection's text formatting, and then press Ctrl+Shift+V to paste, or apply, the copied formatting to a new selection.

Procedure Reference: Copy Text Formatting to Several Text Selections

To copy text formatting and apply it to several other text selections:

1. Select the text with the formatting you want to copy.
2. On the Standard toolbar, double-click the Format Painter button so the Format Painter will remain active.
3. Drag to select the first text selection to apply the copied text formatting.
4. Repeat step 3 as needed.
5. When finished applying the copied text formatting, click the Format Painter button to turn off the tool.

ACTIVITY 3-5

Copying and Applying Text Formatting

Setup:

My Relocation Services is open.

Scenario:

When you formatted the text "Relocation Network:", you changed its font, font size, font styles, and applied a text effect. You would like to apply it to the remaining headings, but don't want to start all over again with each one.

What You Do | **How You Do It**

1. **Copy the text formatting from "Relocation Network:"**

   a. Near the top of the document, **select "Relocation Network:"**

   RELOCATION NETWORK:

   b. On the Standard toolbar, **click the Format Painter button** **once** to copy the selection's text formatting.

   Notice that the mouse pointer changes into an I-beam with a paint brush, indicating that the Format Painter is active.

2. **Apply the formatting to "Relocation Package:"**

   a. At the beginning of the next paragraph, **drag to select "Relocation Package:"** to apply the copied text formatting.

   b. **Deselect the text.**

   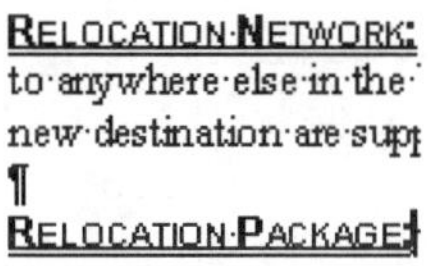
   RELOCATION·NETWORK:
to·anywhere·else·in·the·
new·destination·are·sup
¶
RELOCATION·PACKAGE:

   The mouse pointer has reverted back to an I-beam because the Format Painter is no longer active.

3. **Apply the text formatting from "Relocation Package:" to the remaining four inline headings.**

   a. **Select "Relocation Package:"**

   b. **Double-click the Format Painter button** so it will remain active until turned off.

   c. **Drag to select "Relocation Team:"** to apply the copied text formatting.

   d. With the Format Painter still active, **select "Sales Associates:"**

   e. **Select "Corporate Division:" then "Our Guarantee:"** to finish applying the copied text formatting.

   f. **Click the Format Painter button once** to turn it off.

   g. **Deselect the text.**

TOPIC F

Clear Formatting

Fonts, sizes, styles, effects, and colors are all ways to format text. However, too much text formatting can be distracting. In this topic, you will clear some text formatting.

You are sent a document that contains too much text formatting—everything is bold or underlined, at least a dozen colors, and there doesn't seem to be any rhyme or reason for the variety of fonts and font sizes. The text is difficult to read so the document's message is drowning in a sea of unnecessary formatting. To rescue the document's message, you could try to remove each formatting option that was used, but that would take a long time and you may miss a couple instances here and there. (Undo won't work because when the document was closed, the Undo list was cleared.) You could retype the text in a new blank document, but that would waste valuable time. Word can remove formatting, leaving only the text, so you have more time to edit or format it as you see fit.

Reveal Formatting Task Pane

The Reveal Formatting task pane makes it easy to identify the specific formatting options applied to a text selection. (See Figure 3-4.) To display a selection's formatting options, choose Format→Reveal Formatting.

Rather than selecting text, you can also place the insertion point in the text that contains the formatting you want to identify.

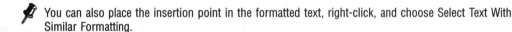

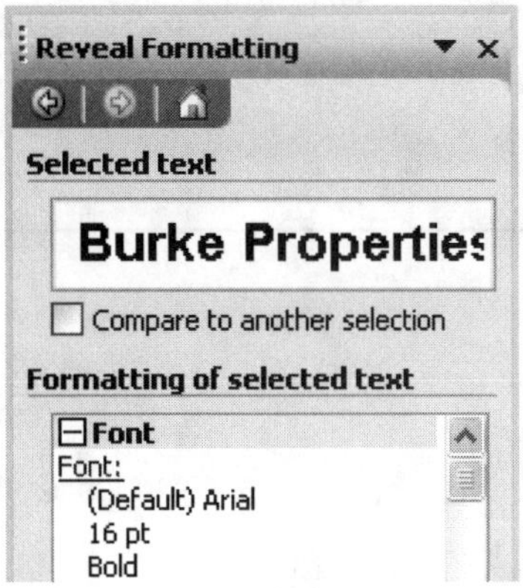

Figure 3-4: *The Reveal Formatting task pane.*

Select Text with Similar Formatting

When you want to select all instances of similarly formatted text:

1. Select the text that contains the desired formatting.
2. If necessary, display the Reveal Formatting task pane.
3. In the Reveal Formatting task pane, place your mouse pointer over the Selected Text box and click the down arrow.
4. Select the Select All Text With Similar Formatting option.

You can also place the insertion point in the formatted text, right-click, and choose Select Text With Similar Formatting.

Once similar text is selected, you can modify all of the selections at the same time.

How to Clear Formatting

Procedure Reference: Clear Formatting Using the Reveal Formatting Task Pane

To clear text formats:

1. Select the text that contains the formatting you want to clear.
2. Choose View→Task Pane and select Reveal Formatting from the Task Pane drop-down list box.

   Use Reveal Formatting to see which text formats are applied.

3. Place your mouse pointer over the Selected Text box and click the down arrow.
4. Select Clear Formatting.

   Note that clearing text formatting does not remove highlighting. You need to turn off highlighting separately using the Highlight button.

Other Ways to Clear Formatting

The benefit of using the Reveal Formatting task pane to clear text formatting is that the task pane shows how the text is currently formatted. If it doesn't matter how a text selection is formatted, you can reset its character formatting.

- Choose Edit→Clear→Formats.

- Or, press Ctrl+Spacebar.

ACTIVITY 3-6

Clearing Text Formatting

Setup:

My Relocation Services is open.

Scenario:

The highlighted text in the last paragraph in the Relocation Services document now contains redundant formatting. Since the highlighting now serves the purpose that the italic and green text formats once did, you decide to clear some of the unnecessary formatting.

What You Do	How You Do It
1. **Select "unconditionally guarantee" and display the Reveal Formatting task pane.**	a. In the highlighted text of the last paragraph, **select "unconditionally guarantee."**
	b. **Choose View→Task Pane.**
	c. From near the bottom of the Task Pane drop-down list box, **select Reveal Formatting.**

2. **In the Reveal Formatting task pane's Formatting Of Selected Text list box, the font attributes include: (Default) Times New Roman, 12 pt, and____ .**

3. **The only Character Options listed in the Formatting Of Selected Text list box is________ .**

4. **Clear the formatting from the selected text.**

a. In the Reveal Formatting task pane, in the Selected Text box, **place your mouse pointer over "unconditionally" and click the down arrow** to display a drop-down list box of options.

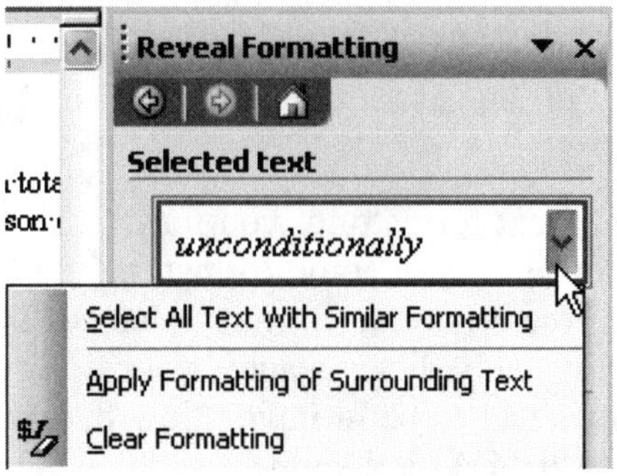

b. **Select Clear Formatting.**

---

5. **Using the Reveal Formatting task pane, which Font attribute was cleared?**_____

---

6. **True or False? The highlighting was cleared, too.**

__ True

__ False

---

7. **Clear the green font color from "money back" and deselect the text.**

a. In the same paragraph, **select "money back."**

Font Color: Green is displayed in the task pane's Formatting Of Selected Text list box.

b. From the Selected Text drop-down list box, **select Clear Formatting.**

c. **Deselect the text.**

---

8. **Close the Reveal Formatting task pane.**

TOPIC G

Find and Replace Text Formatting

Text formatting decisions are often made on the spot. As you finish your document, formatting choices may no longer seem appropriate. In this topic, you will find and replace some text formatting.

As you apply text formatting, you may make a variety of decisions that may need to be changed later. However, some formatting may be subtle and difficult to locate each and every instance. Or, there may be so many changes that it would take a long time to make the changes individually. For instance, your department style guidelines used to require that all product names had to be in italic. Now the requirement has changed and all product names have to be in bold. In a document such as the monthly catalog, which contains hundreds of product names, those changes are quite substantial. Rather than scroll through a document trying to locate specific text formatting and potentially missing a few instances, you can let Word locate and replace all instances quickly and easily, minimizing the effort you need to exert while still getting thorough results.

How to Find and Replace Text Formatting

Procedure Reference: Find and Replace Text Formatting

To find and replace text formatting in your document:

1. Move the insertion point to the top of the document.
2. Display the Replace tab in the Find And Replace dialog box. (Choose Edit→Replace.)
3. With the insertion point in the Find What text box, delete unwanted text and formatting options.
4. If necessary, set Find Font options.
   a. Click the More button.
   b. In the Replace area, click Format and select Font to display the Find Font dialog box.
   c. Select the desired font attributes you want to find.
   d. Click OK.
5. Move the insertion point in the Replace With text box, and delete unwanted text and formatting options.
6. If necessary, set Replace Font options.
   a. If necessary, click the More button to show the Replace options.
   b. Click Format and select Font to display the Replace Font dialog box.
   c. Select the desired font attributes you want to replace.
   d. Click OK.
7. Click Find Next to begin the search, replacing instances as needed.

If you change your mind about a replace operation, click the Undo button on the Standard toolbar. If you used the Replace button, Word will undo the replacements one by one. If you used the Replace All button, Word will undo all of the replacements at once.

8. When Word has finished searching for text formatting in the document, click OK.
9. Close the Find And Replace dialog box.

Procedure Reference: Remove Formats from the Find And Replace Dialog Box

To remove formats from the Find What and Replace With text boxes in the Find And Replace dialog box:

1. Place the insertion point in the text box that contains the format(s) you want to remove.
2. Click More to display the Search and Replace options.
3. Click No Formatting to remove the formats from the text box.
4. If necessary, remove the formats from the other text box.

Tips for Removing Formats

When you display the Replace tab, some font formats may already be displayed under the Find What and Replace With text boxes, perhaps left over from a previous task. Before you begin a new search, you should remove the formats so they don't interfere with your new search.

ACTIVITY 3-7

Finding and Replacing Text Formatting

Setup:

My Relocation Services is open.

Scenario:

Your co-worker suggests some cosmetic changes to your document. To give the text a more unique look, she suggests changing the font. She also mentions how bad the bold and double-underline looks in the inline headings. You decide to take her advice because she has a good sense of design.

What You Do | **How You Do It**

1. With the insertion point at the top of the document, **display the Replace tab in the Find And Replace dialog box and set Arial as the font format that you want to find.**

   a. **Move the insertion point to the top of the document.**

   b. **Display the Replace tab in the Find And Replace dialog box.**

      Choose Edit→Replace.

   c. **Delete any text from the Find What text box.**

   d. **Click More.**

   e. In the Replace section at the bottom of the dialog box, **click Format and select Font** to display the Find Font dialog box.

   f. From the Font text box, **type *Arial* and click OK.**

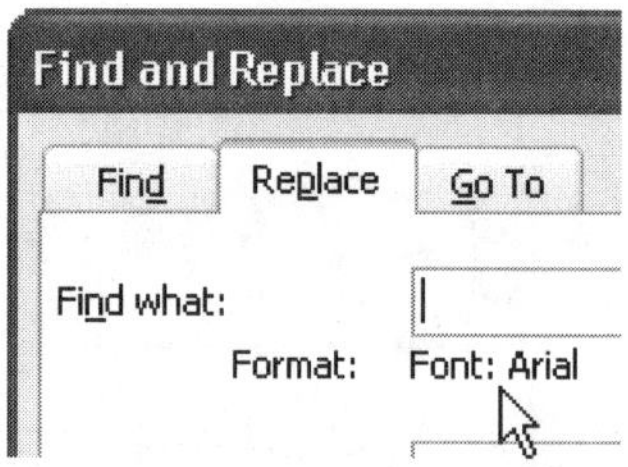

---

2. **Set Tahoma as the font format that you want to replace Arial with.**

   a. **Place the insertion point in the Replace With text box.**

   b. **Delete any text from the Replace With text box.**

   c. **Click Format and select Font.**

   d. In the Font text box, **type *Tahoma* and click OK.** The Format is listed under the Replace With text box.

   e. **Click Less.**

3. **Replace all instances of Arial with Tahoma without confirming the changes.**	a. **Click Replace All.** b. When Word has completed its search, **click OK.** All text formatted with Arial has been changed to Tahoma.
4. **Clear the font formats from both the Find What and Replace With text boxes.**	a. If necessary, **place the insertion point in the Find What text box.** b. **Click More.** c. Near the bottom of the dialog box, **click No Formatting.** d. **Place the insertion point in the Replace With text box and click No Formatting.**
5. **Set Bold and Double Underline as the Find Font options.**	a. **Place the insertion point in the Find What text box.** b. **Click Format and select Font** to display the Find Font dialog box. c. In the Font Style list box, **select Bold.** d. From the Underline Style drop-down list box, **select the Double Underline option.** e. **Click OK.** When you select the Double Underline option, it is displayed below the Find What text box.

6. **Set Regular and (None) as the Replace Font options.**

   If you do not specify formatting in the Replace With text box, all the bold, double-underlined text will essentially be deleted.

   a. **Place the insertion point in the Replace With text box.**

   b. **Click Format and select Font.**

   c. In the Font Style list box, **select Regular.**

   d. From the Underline Style drop-down list box, **select the (None) option.**

   e. **Click OK.**

   f. **Click Less.**

7. **Replace all instances of the specified formatting without confirming the changes.**

   a. **Click Replace All.**

   b. When Word has completed its search, **click OK.**

   All bold and underlined text has been replaced with regular non-underlined text. All Arial, bold, and double-underlined formatting has been replaced by regular Tahoma with no underlining.

   c. **Close the Find And Replace dialog box.**

8. **Save and close the document.**

Lesson 3 Follow-up

In this lesson, you learned how to make text selections stand out from surrounding text by adding visual interest as well as enhancing your text's message. To do that, you changed fonts and font sizes to increase readability. You applied font styles and effects, such as bold, italic, and small caps. You then changed font colors and highlighted text to add some color as well as to point out important text. Once you had text formatted the way you wanted it, you used the Format Painter to copy the formatting from one text selection to another. With some formatting no longer necessary, you cleared the formatting. Lastly, you used the Find And Replace dialog box to locate and replace specific text formatting with new formats.

1. **How will you use text formatting to improve your documents?**

2. **How might you use the Find And Replace dialog box to save you time when formatting your text?**

NOTES

LESSON 4
Formatting Paragraphs

Lesson Time
50 minutes

Lesson Objectives:

In this lesson, you will format paragraphs.

You will:

- Set tab stops.
- Align paragraphs horizontally.
- Indent paragraphs.
- Add borders and shading to paragraphs.
- Apply a style to text.
- Create a bulleted and a numbered list.
- Change paragraph spacing.

Introduction

In the previous lesson, you applied character formatting to existing text. This lesson will introduce you to Word's paragraph formatting options.

Consider two documents: one without paragraph formatting and one with paragraph formatting. (See Figure 4-1.)

Burke Annual Report
Fiscal Year & Accomplishments
This fiscal year was truly a foundation-building year for Burke Properties, Inc. Fueled by a continued strong economy and robust commercial real estate markets, we significantly increased our revenues and earnings, strengthened our balance sheet, and put in place a solid platform from which we can now aggressively implement our long-term growth strategy.

Burke
Annual Report

Fiscal Year & Accomplishments

This fiscal year was truly a foundation-building year for Burke Properties, Inc. Fueled by a continued strong economy and robust commercial real estate markets, we:

- Significantly increased our revenues and earnings.
- Strengthened our balance sheet.
- Put in place a solid platform from which we can now aggressively implement our long-term growth strategy.

Figure 4-1: *A document without paragraph (left) and one with paragraph formatting (right).*

It's clear which is easier to read and understand! By formatting the paragraphs in your documents, you can enhance their readability and visual appeal.

TOPIC A

Set Tabs

You have already used Word's default tab settings. However, these may not always suit your needs. In this topic, you will customize the default tab settings.

Your division manager wants you to provide him with a document containing the company's e-commerce data for the last three years. You begin entering the data in a document, pressing the Spacebar to separate the data from the yearly labels. It looks good to you, so you send it to him. Unfortunately, he applies a different font to the data to make it blend in with the rest of his document. The data, which used to be aligned neatly, becomes a disorderly mess, making it difficult to follow. Using tabs rather than spaces would have saved you the embarrassment. (See Figure 4-2.)

```
Web·Sales¶
Last·Three·Years¶
·········Q1·····Q2·····Q3·····Q4¶
2000···12.1···32.2···42.3···44.9¶
2001···55.8···66.9···78.7···74.7¶
2002··100.7··112.4··110.4··201.8¶
```

```
Web·Sales¶
Last·Three·Years¶
·····Q1·····Q2·····Q3·····Q4¶
2000·····12.1·····32.2·····42.3·····44.9¶
2001·····55.8·····66.9·····78.7·····74.7¶
2002·····100.7·····112.4·····110.4·····201.8¶
```

Figure 4-2: *When spaces are used instead of tabs to mimic columns, the text's appearance can be affected if fonts change.*

Tabs

Tabs, or *tab stops*, enable you to line up text to the left, right, center, or to a decimal character or bar character.

Types of Tab Stops

There are five types of tab stops you can use. Table 4-1 describes these.

By default, tab stops are left-aligned and set at 0.5-inch increments.

Table 4-1: *Tab Stops*

Tab Name	Tab Stop Button	Description
Left tab		Text flows to the right of the tab stop.
Center tab		Text is centered on the tab stop.
Right tab		Text flows to the left of the tab stop.
Decimal tab		Text aligns on the decimal point (used for numbers).
Bar tab		Adds a vertical line at the tab stop.

Holding down the Alt key as you drag tabs will display detailed measurements in the ruler.

Margins

A *margin* is the area of white space along the top, bottom, left, and right edges of a page. Margins determine the size of the document's text area. The larger the margins, the smaller the text area.

By default, a new blank document has 1-inch margins at the top and bottom, and 1.25-inch left and right side margins.

A document's left margin also doubles as the selection bar.

How to Set Tab Stops

Procedure Reference: Set a Tab Stop on the Ruler

To set a tab stop on the horizontal ruler:

1. Select the paragraph(s) that will contain the tab stop.
2. Select the type of tab you want to set by clicking the Tab Stop button [L] (to the left of the horizontal ruler and just above the vertical ruler).

   If you want to set tabs for only one paragraph, rather than select the paragraph, you can just place the insertion point in it.

   The type of tab you select remains active until you change it, so you can set several similar tabs quickly.

3. Point to the desired tab-stop position on the horizontal ruler, and click the mouse button to set the tab stop.

Procedure Reference: Move a Tab Stop

Once you set a tab stop, you can easily adjust its position on the horizontal ruler. To move a tab stop:

1. Select the paragraph(s) that contain the tab stop you want to move.
2. Click and drag the existing tab stop to a new location on the ruler.

Procedure Reference: Clear a Tab Stop

Tab stops can easily be cleared, or removed, from the horizontal ruler. To do so:

1. Select the paragraph(s) that contain the tab stop you want to remove.
2. Click and drag the existing tab stop down and off the ruler.

Tabs Dialog Box

You can also set and clear tabs using the Tabs dialog box. (Double-click a tab stop on the ruler or choose Format→Tabs.) This method gives you the ability to specify tab stop positions exactly, change default tab stop positions, choose a leader character for the tab, as well as clear all tab stops from a paragraph.

Leader Characters

Leader characters are solid, dotted, or dashed lines that fill the tabbed space between text when a tab has been inserted. They can be added using the Tabs dialog box.

ACTIVITY 4-1

Setting Tab Stops with the Ruler

Data Files:

- Meeting Topics.doc

Setup:

No documents are open.

Scenario:

Your manager put you in charge of collecting regional data for the next quarterly sales meeting. You've already entered the data in the Meeting Topics memo; however, you should make sure it is aligned properly.

What You Do	How You Do It
1. At the top of the meeting topics memo, **set a left tab stop at 1.25 inches.**	a. **Open Meeting Topics.**
	b. **Select the Attention, From, and Regarding paragraphs.**

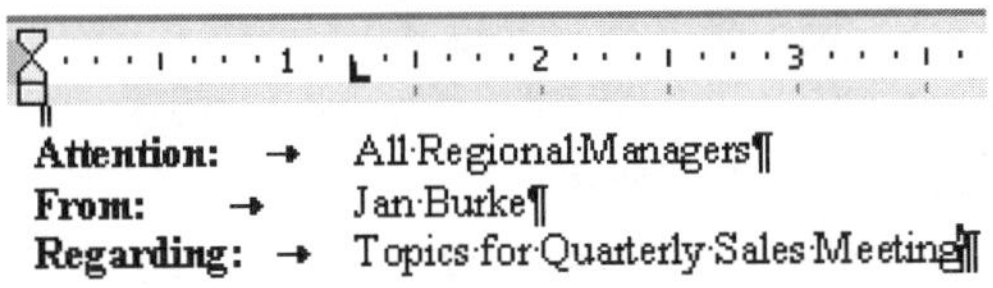

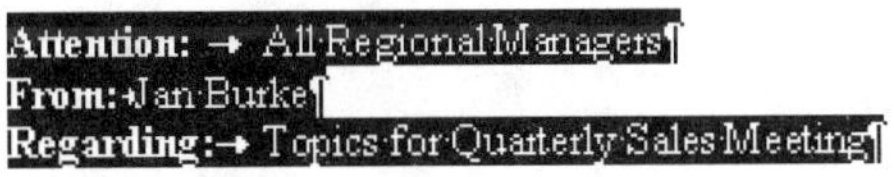

c. With the left tab stop displayed on the Tab Stop button, **place the mouse pointer over the horizontal ruler at 1.25 inches and click the mouse button** to set the left tab stop.

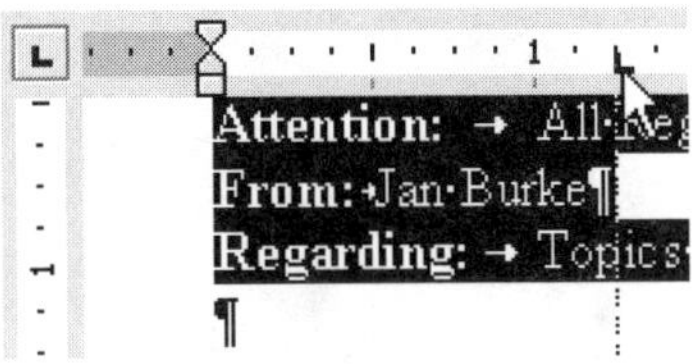

d. **Deselect the text.**

What You Do	How You Do It
2. In the quarterly tabbed data, there is a center tab at the 2-inch mark. **Clear the center tab.**	a. **Select the four paragraphs Month through March.**

b. On the horizontal ruler, **click and drag the center tab stop off the horizontal ruler.**

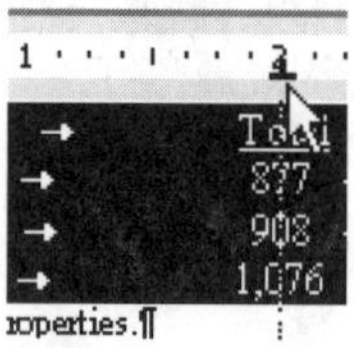

3. For the data, **set a right tab stop at every inch from 1 inch through 6 inches.**

a. With the quarterly tabbed data still selected, **click the Tab Stop button twice until the right tab is displayed.**

b. **Place the mouse pointer over the horizontal ruler at 1 inch and click the mouse button** to set the first right tab stop.

c. **Place a right tab stop at 2 inches, 3 inches, 4 inches, 5 inches, and 5.5 inches.**

d. **Drag the right tab from 5.5 inches to 6 inches.**

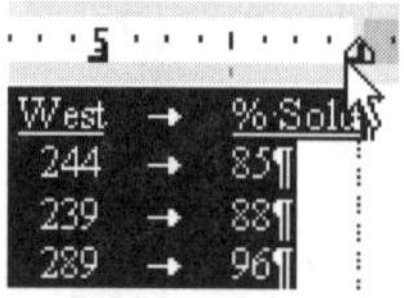

When setting a tab stop at the right margin, it's often easier to set it near the margin and then drag the tab stop into place.

e. **Deselect the text.**

4. **Save the document as *My Meeting Topics*.**

TOPIC B

Change Paragraph Alignment

Character formatting is one way to add emphasis to text. Changing the text's horizontal position on the page is another way to attract attention to text. In this topic, you will position text horizontally between the left and right edges of the page.

You sent out a memo requesting all department members attend the new project kick-off meeting. In the memo, after describing what the meeting would cover, you added the meeting's date, time, and location after the description. As a result, some people didn't notice when and where the meeting was supposed to be so attendance was poor and you had to schedule a second meeting. Offsetting the critical information from the rest of the text would have made it easier for the co-workers to see when the meeting was.

Paragraph Alignment

Paragraph alignment determines how a paragraph is positioned horizontally between the left and right margins or indents. Paragraph alignment options include, align left, center, align right, and justify.

Paragraph Alignment Options

Table 4-2 describes the four paragraph alignment options.

Table 4-2: *Paragraph Alignment Options*

Alignment	Button	Description
Align Left		The left edge of the paragraph is aligned along the left margin or indent. The paragraph's right edge appears ragged.
Center		Both sides of the paragraph are equidistant from left and right margins or indents. Both the left and right edges of the paragraph appear ragged.
Align Right		The right edge of the paragraph is aligned along the right margin or indent. The paragraph's left edge appears ragged.
Justify		Both sides of the paragraph are evenly aligned along the left and right margins or indents. The paragraph's left and right edges are not ragged. Word adjusts the spacing between words so that they stretch from the left margin or indent to the right margin or indent. When the last line of a justified paragraph is short, however, it won't be stretched.

How to Change Paragraph Alignment

Procedure Reference: Change Paragraph Alignment

To change how a paragraph is aligned on a page:

1. Select the paragraph(s) you want to align.

   If you want to change the alignment for only one paragraph, rather than select the paragraph, you can just place the insertion point in it.

2. Apply the desired paragraph alignment.
   - To left align the paragraph, click the Align Left button on the Formatting toolbar, or press Ctrl+L.
   - To right align the paragraph, click the Align Right button on the Formatting toolbar, or press Ctrl+R.
   - To center align the paragraph, click the Center button on the Formatting toolbar, or press Ctrl+E.
   - Or, to justify the paragraph, click the Justify button on the Formatting toolbar, or press Ctrl+J.

ACTIVITY 4-2

Aligning Paragraphs

Setup:

My Meeting Topics is open.

Scenario:

Inserting the right tab stops made you want to change the alignment of some paragraphs in your memo—in particular the alignment of Regional Memo and the quarterly data title and subtitle.

What You Do	How You Do It
1. **Right align "Regional Memo."**	a. At the top of the document, **place the insertion point in the "Regional Memo" title.** b. On the Formatting toolbar, **click the Align Right button** . You may need to use the Formatting toolbar's Toolbar Options button to locate the Align Right button.

2. **Center align the title and subtitle over the quarterly data.**

   a. Above the quarterly data, **select the "Houses Sold by Region" and "First-Quarter Data..." paragraphs.**

   b. On the Formatting toolbar, **click the Center button** .

TOPIC C

Indent Paragraphs

Alignment and tabs are ways to offset text horizontally between the margins. Another way to offset text is to control its left and right boundaries between the margins. In this topic, you will adjust a paragraph's left and right indents.

Indents can make paragraphs more readable as well as provide a way to offset critical ideas. (See Figure 4-3.)

Among our fiscal accomplishments, Burke Properties achieved amazing growth. Here are some highlights: 1. Burke erased all long-term debt. 2. We improved our equity. 3. The company created 100 new jobs.	Among our fiscal accomplishments, Burke Properties achieved amazing growth. Here are some highlights: 1. Burke erased all long-term debt. 2. We improved our equity. 3. The company created 100 new jobs.

Figure 4-3: *Paragraphs without indents (left) can be more difficult to read than indented paragraphs (right).*

Indents

Indents are a way to align a paragraph's left and right edges without changing the margins for the entire document. At the edges of the horizontal ruler are four indent markers that reflect the active paragraph's indentation: first line, hanging, left, and right.

By default, a document's indents are set equal with the document's left and right margins.

Types of Indent Markers

Table 4-3 describes the individual indent markers.

Table 4-3: ***Indent Markers***

Horizontal Ruler Icon	Description
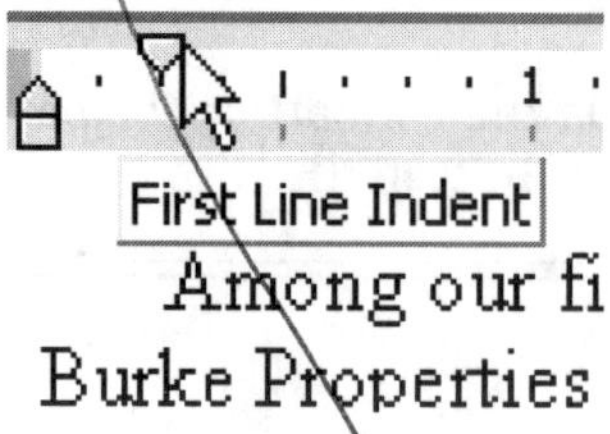	First Line Indent marker controls the left boundary for the first line of a paragraph.
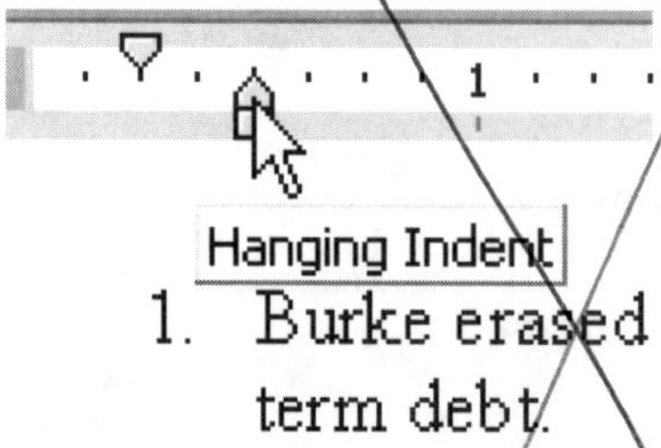	Hanging Indent marker controls the left boundary of every line in a paragraph, except the first line.
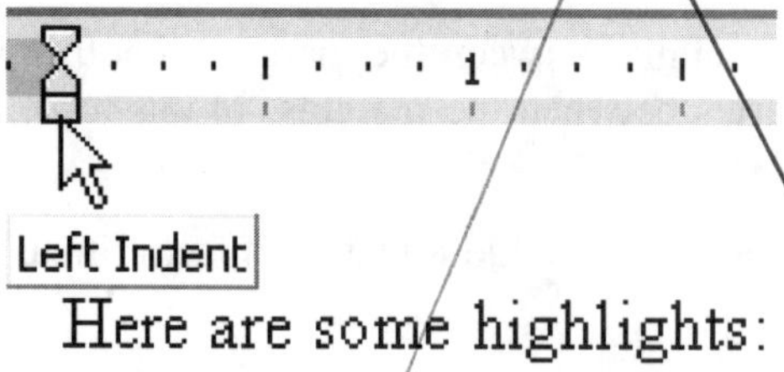	Left Indent marker controls the left boundary for every line in a paragraph, except when a First Line or Hanging Indent has been applied. When no left-margin indents are applied, moving the Left Indent marker simultaneously moves the First Line and Hanging Indent markers.
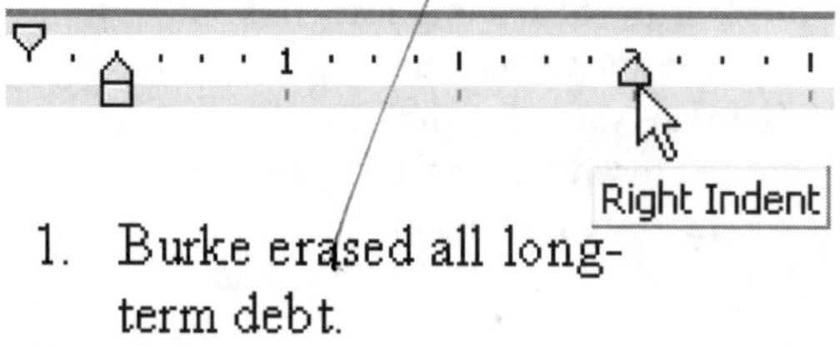	Right Indent marker controls the right boundary for every line in a paragraph, regardless of left-side indents.

How to Indent Paragraphs

Procedure Reference: Indent Paragraphs Using the Formatting Toolbar

To use these buttons to modify the left indent:

The Increase and Decrease Indent buttons do not affect first line, hanging, or right indents.

1. Select the paragraph(s) you want to indent.
2. Set the desired left indent.
    - To indent the paragraph 0.5-inch increments to the right at a time, click the Increase Indent button .

      Press Ctrl+M to increase the indent.

    - Or, to decrease the indent by the same amount, click the Decrease Indent button .

easy

to make tool bars bigger right click blue screen properties settings move lever to left okay

Press Ctrl+Shift+M to decrease the indent.

Procedure Reference: Indent Paragraphs Using the Ruler

To indent a paragraph using the ruler:

Indenting paragraphs using the ruler is best suited for making quick adjustments to both the left and right indents, when precision doesn't matter.

1. Select the paragraph(s) you want to indent.
2. Drag the appropriate indent marker(s) to a new position on the horizontal ruler.

Procedure Reference: Indent Paragraphs Using the Paragraph Dialog Box

To indent a paragraph using the Paragraph dialog box:

1. Select the paragraph(s) you want to indent.
2. Choose Format→Paragraph to display the Paragraph dialog box.
3. On the Indents And Spacing tab, change the Indentation settings.

Use Accurate Indentation Measurements

Setting indents using the ruler can be a little tricky because the indent markers are quite small and it can be difficult to position them exactly where you want them. Using the Increase and Decrease Indent buttons limits you to 0.5 inch increments and only affects the left indent. So when you need to position indent markers accurately, use the Indentation area of the Paragraph dialog box.

ACTIVITY 4-3

Indenting Paragraphs

Setup:

My Meeting Topics is open.

Scenario:

In the memo, rather than standing out as a specific block of text that needs to be reviewed, the disclaimer text blends into the memo. You need to make the disclaimer more identifiable.

What You Do	How You Do It

1. **Set the left indent to 1 inch for the four disclaimer-related paragraphs.**

a. **Select the four disclaimer-related paragraphs, from "Disclaimer" through "... constitute or imply an endorsement."**

b. On the Formatting toolbar, **click the Increase Indent button** .

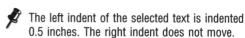

The left indent of the selected text is indented 0.5 inches. The right indent does not move.

c. **Click the Increase Indent button again** to set the left indent at 1 inch.

2. **Set the disclaimer text's right indent to 1 inch.**

a. With the four disclaimer-related paragraphs still selected, **locate the Right Indent marker on the horizontal ruler.**

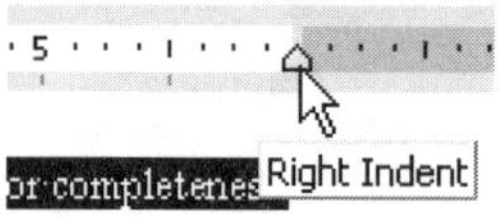

If you deselect the disclaimer paragraphs, be sure to reselect them before moving the Right Indent marker.

b. **Click and drag the Right Indent marker to the left one inch, so it is positioned at the 5-inch mark.**

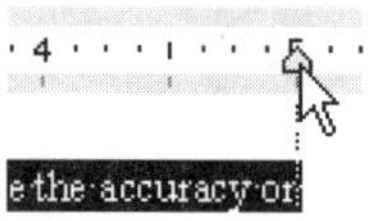

As you drag the Right Indent marker, notice the vertical guide displayed in the text area.

c. **Deselect the text.**

3. **Indent the first line of the "Errors," "Responsibility," and "Endorsement" paragraphs 0.25 inches.**

a. **Select the "Errors," "Responsibility," and "Endorsement" paragraphs.**

b. On the horizontal ruler, at the 1-inch mark, **locate the First Line Indent marker for the selected text.**

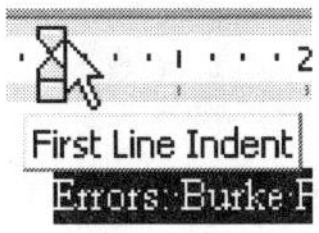

The First Line Indent marker is the downward-pointing indent marker.

c. **Drag the First Line Indent marker to the right 0.25 inches.**

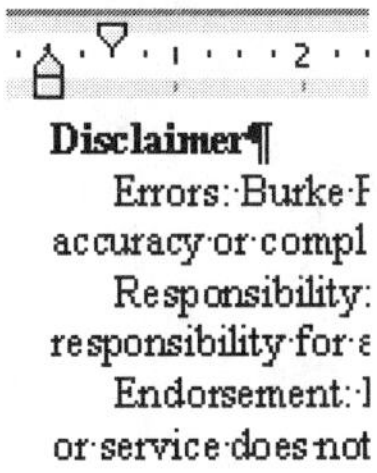

The selected paragraphs now have a first-line indent of 0.5 inches. Again, the margins remain the same.

d. **Deselect the text.**

TOPIC D

Add Borders and Shading

Once you have your paragraphs in the desired position, you may want to dress them up a little. In this topic, you will add borders and shading to paragraphs.

The visual interest provided by shaded paragraphs with borders helps the reader locate critical ideas quickly just by skimming the document, because the formatted paragraph clearly stands out from the surrounding text. Figure 4-4 shows a paragraph without and with borders and shading.

Disclaimer: Burke Properties does not guarantee the accuracy of its published information.	**Disclaimer:** Burke Properties does not guarantee the accuracy of its published information.

Figure 4-4: *A paragraph without borders and shading (left) and the same paragraph with borders and shading (right).*

Borders and Shading

Definition:

A *border* is a decorative line or pattern that is displayed around an object, such as a paragraph, picture, or page. *Shading* is a percentage of color that can be added to the background of an object, like text, paragraph, or table data. Both borders and shading can be used to draw attention to the object to which they are applied.

Borders and shading can also be applied to small text selections (a word, phrase, or sentence).

Example:

Eastern Regional Memo

Attention:	All Eastern Regional Managers
From:	Jan Burke
Regarding:	Topics for Quarterly Sales Meeting

Figure 4-5: *Borders and shading help draw attention to text.*

Custom Borders

Borders do not need to surround a paragraph. Using the Custom setting in the Borders And Shading dialog box, you can click the top, bottom, left, or right borders to add and remove them.

How to Add Borders and Shading to a Paragraph

Procedure Reference: Add a Border Using the Borders Button

The fastest way to apply a black-line border to a paragraph is to use the Borders button on the Formatting toolbar. To do that:

1. Select the paragraph(s) to which you want to add a border.
2. Apply a border.
   - To apply an outside border, click the Borders button on the Formatting toolbar.
   - Or, to apply a customized border, click the drop-down arrow on the Borders button and select the border you want to apply.

You may need to use the Formatting toolbar's Toolbar Options button to locate the Borders button.

Procedure Reference: Add a Border Using the Borders And Shading Dialog Box

To add a border to a paragraph using this method:

For more control over border appearance, use the Borders And Shading dialog box.

1. Select the paragraph(s) to which you want to add a border.
2. Choose Format→Borders And Shading to display the Borders And Shading dialog box.
3. Select the Borders tab.
4. Select a Setting (None, Box, Shadow, 3-D, or Custom).
5. If desired, select a different Style, Color, and/or Width for the border.
6. Use the Preview area to verify that the borders look the way you want them to. If necessary, in the Preview area, click the border buttons to add or remove them.

   If you also want to apply shading to the same paragraph, rather than click OK, you can select the Shading tab and make those settings now as well.

7. Click OK to apply the border.

Procedure Reference: Add Shading Using the Borders And Shading Dialog Box

To add shade to a paragraph:

1. Select the paragraph(s) you want to shade.
2. Choose Format→Borders And Shading to display the Borders And Shading dialog box.
3. Select the Shading tab.
4. From the Fill palette, select an appropriate Fill color.
   - If you don't see a color you want, select More Colors.
   - Or, if you want to remove shading, click No Fill.

5. If necessary, from the Style drop-down list, select a shading percentage or pattern.
6. Use the Preview area to verify that the shading looks the way you want it.
7. Click OK to apply the shading.

ACTIVITY 4-4

Applying Borders and Shading to a Paragraph

Setup:

My Meeting Topics is open.

Scenario:

Aligning and indenting paragraphs doesn't offset the text quite enough. You need to make these paragraphs stand out more, so you decide to apply borders and shading.

What You Do	How You Do It
1. **Apply a bottom border to the "Regional Memo" title.**	a. **Place the insertion point in the "Regional Memo" title.**
	b. On the Formatting toolbar, **click the drop-down arrow on the Borders button** to display other types of borders. 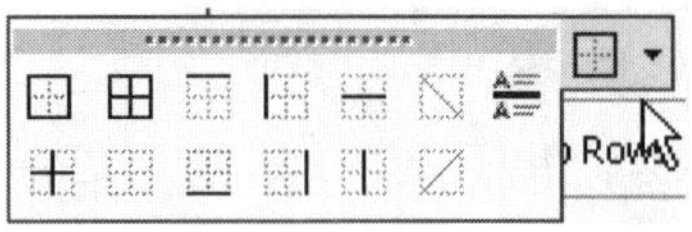
	c. **Select Bottom Border** to place a single-line border below the "Regional Memo" title. The bottom border extends from the Left Indent marker to the Right Indent marker. 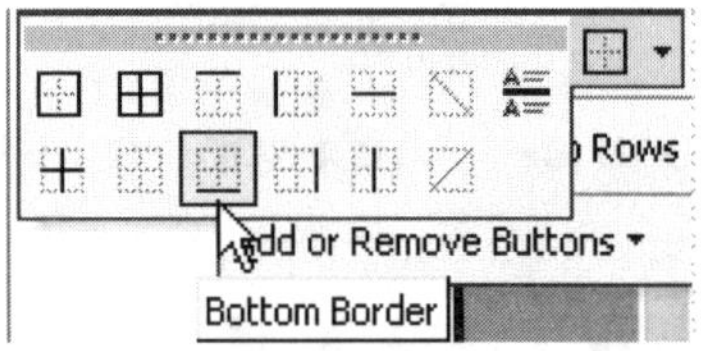

2. **Box the quarterly data paragraphs.**

a. **Select the paragraphs from "Houses Sold by Region" through "Source: Burke Properties."**

b. **Choose Format→Borders And Shading** to display the Borders tab in the Borders And Shading dialog box.

c. On the Borders tab, under Setting, **select Box.**

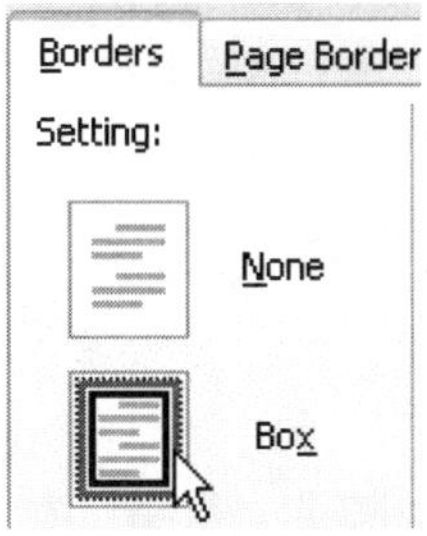

d. **Notice the Preview area.** The Box selection will apply a black, half point outside border around the selected paragraphs.

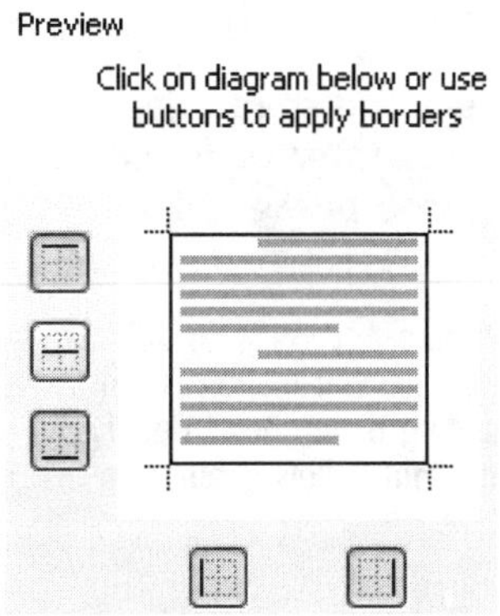

---

3. **Apply a light yellow shading to the quarterly data paragraphs.**

⚠ If you closed the Borders And Shading dialog box, redisplay it (Format→Borders And Shading).

a. With the Borders And Shading dialog box still displayed, **select the Shading tab.**

b. Under Fill, **select Light Yellow.**

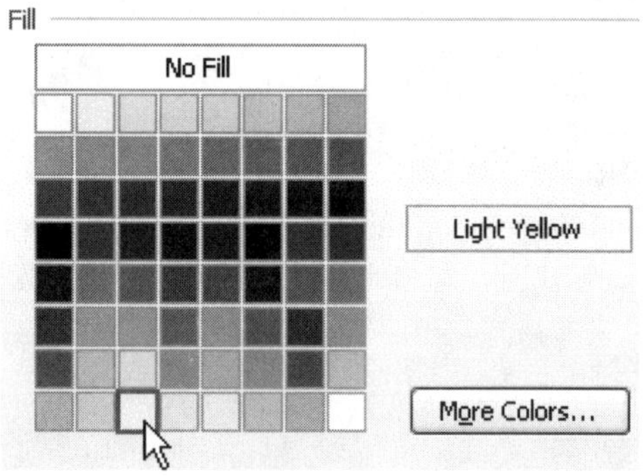

c. **Click OK** to apply the border and shading options.

The top and bottom borders extend from the Left Indent marker to the Right Indent marker.

d. **Deselect the text.**

Do not perform any other actions after deselecting the text.

4. **Repeat the borders and shading options for the disclaimer title and the subsequent three paragraphs.**

If the Repeat Borders And Shading option is not available on the Edit menu, use the Borders And Shading dialog box to apply a box border and light yellow shading to the disclaimer text.

a. **Select the four disclaimer-related paragraphs, from "Disclaimer" through "... constitute or imply an endorsement."**

b. **Choose Edit→Repeat Borders And Shading** to apply the same border and shading options to the disclaimer text.

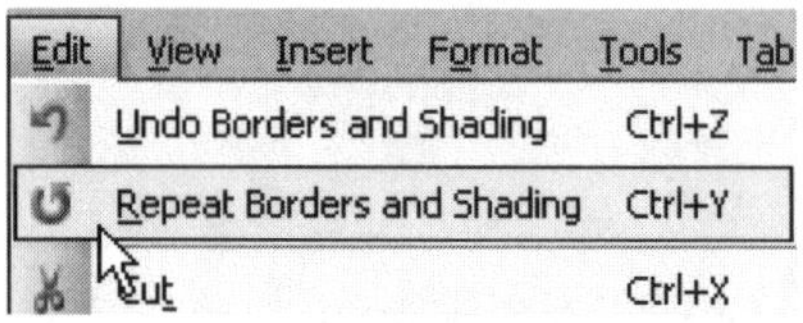

---

5. **The disclaimer text's top and bottom borders extend to the Left and Right _____ _____, not the left and right margins.**

---

6. **Save and close My Meeting Topics.**

TOPIC E

Apply Styles

So far you have applied various text formatting options one at a time. To reuse those formats, you either had to repeat each formatting option or use the Format Painter. In this topic, you will apply several formatting options simultaneously by using Word's default styles.

You have a document with 20 major headings and each one needs to be formatted as Arial, bold, 16 point, with a half-inch indent. You could set the font and paragraph attributes 20 different times. But you may forget to change one of the attributes. Of course, you could format one heading then reuse the formatting with the Format Painter, but that's still not the most efficient way. The best way to ensure that you apply formatting easily and consistently is to store the desired attributes together so that they can be applied all at once with the click of a button. Word's style feature allows you to do just that!

Styles

Definition:

A *style* is a set of formatting instructions that is stored under one name. When the style is applied, all of the formatting instructions are applied to text simultaneously and consistently with little effort.

Example:

Table 4-4: *Common Styles*

Style	Font and Paragraph Formatting Included
Heading 1	Arial, 16 pt, bold, left aligned, no indentation.
Heading 2	Arial, 14 pt, bold, italic, left aligned, no indentation.
Heading 3	Arial, 13 pt, bold, left aligned, no indentation.
Normal	Times New Roman, 12 pt, left aligned, no indentation.

Paragraph and Character Styles

Word includes several types of styles, but the most commonly used ones are either paragraph or character styles. A paragraph style is used to control the appearance of a paragraph and can include paragraph formatting (such as alignment, indentation, borders, and shading) as well as character formatting (such as font, font style, font size, and effects). A character style, sometimes called an inline style, is used to control the appearance of selected text within a paragraph. Character styles include only character formatting—no paragraph formatting.

Word also includes table and list styles.

Styles And Formatting Task Pane

The Style And Formatting task pane can be used to apply and reapply existing styles. It can also be used to:

- Show formatting applied to selected text.
- Select all instances of a particular style.
- Create new styles.
- Clear formatting and styles from selected text.
- View existing styles.

(See Figure 4-6.) To display the task pane, you can click the Styles And Formatting button on the Formatting toolbar.

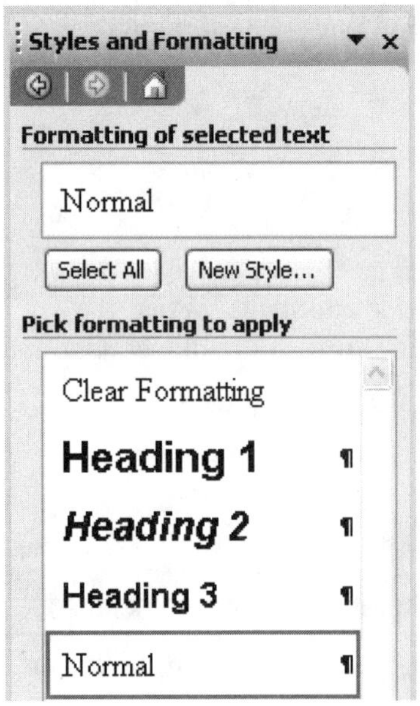

Figure 4-6: *The Styles And Formatting task pane.*

How to Apply a Style

Procedure Reference: Apply a Style

To apply a style:

1. Select the paragraph(s) to which you want to apply a style.

   If you want to apply a character style, select just that text without the paragraph mark.

2. Apply the style.
   - To apply a style from the Style drop-down list Normal on the Formatting toolbar, display the list and select a style.
   - Or, to apply a style from the Styles And Formatting task pane, select a style from the Pick Formatting To Apply list.

ACTIVITY 4-5

Applying Paragraph Styles

Data Files:

- Meeting Agenda.doc

Setup:

No documents are open.

Scenario:

With the meeting topics set, it's time to turn your attention to the meeting agenda. To distinguish between the levels of meeting topics, you decide to apply appropriate heading styles to the title text throughout the document.

What You Do	How You Do It
1. In Meeting Agenda, **apply the first-level heading style to "Quarterly Sales Meeting."**	a. **Open Meeting Agenda.** b. At the top of the page, **place the insertion point in the "Quarterly Sales Meeting" paragraph.** c. On the Formatting toolbar, from the Style box drop-down list, **select Heading 1** to apply the Heading 1 paragraph style. 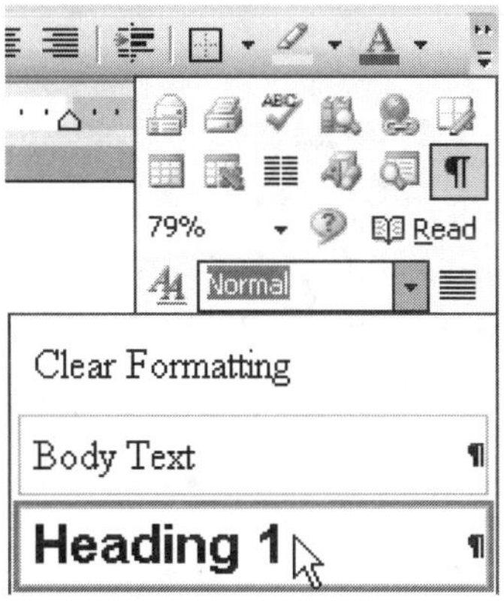

2. **Apply the second-level heading style to the "Agenda" paragraph.**

   a. **Place the insertion point in the "Agenda" paragraph.**

   b. From the Style box drop-down list, **select Heading 2** to apply the style.

3. **Apply the third-level heading style to the "Review Minutes," "Quarterly Home Sales," "Approve New Disclaimer," and "Action Items" paragraphs.**

   a. **Select the "Review Minutes" paragraph.**

   b. Using the selection bar, **press and hold Ctrl while clicking the "Quarterly Home Sales," "Approve New Disclaimer," and "Action Items" paragraphs** to add each to the selection.

   c. To apply the style to all four paragraphs at the same time, from the Style box drop-down list, **select Heading 3.**

4. **Save the document as *My Meeting Agenda*.**

TOPIC F

Create Lists

Indents and tabs are useful ways to offset text on a page. However, they don't offer as much visual interest as they could. In this topic, you will create bulleted and numbered lists.

Which of the following sets of instructions is easier to follow? (See Figure 4-7.)

Driving Directions to Burke from the North

Take Interstate 93 SOUTH to the Callahan Tunnel exit. At the end of the off ramp, go straight through the intersection, following signs for "Waterfront Surface Artery." At the second light, turn right on South Ave. Burke Properties is ahead, about three blocks on the left.

Driving Directions to Burke from the North

1. Take Interstate 93 SOUTH to the Callahan Tunnel exit.
2. At the end of the off ramp, go straight through the intersection, following signs for "Waterfront Surface Artery."
3. At the second light, turn right on South Ave. Burke Properties is ahead, about three blocks on the left.

Figure 4-7: *Instructions in a paragraph (left). Instructions in a list (right).*

Putting information in a list not only enhances how it looks, but lists can also enhance readability. Lists will help your audience properly use the information that you provide.

Lists

Lists are used to present information separately from the surrounding text. Word allows you to create several types of lists, but the most commonly used ones are the bulleted list and the numbered list. A bulleted list is used to denote a group of equally significant items. A numbered list is used to denote a ranking or sequence that must be followed to achieve a desired outcome. (See Figure 4-8.)

You can also create outline numbered lists.

Simple Salsa

Ingredients

- 1½ cups chopped tomatoes
- 4 oz. sliced green onions
- 3 tbsp. cilantro
- 2 tbsp. lemon juice
- 2 jalapeno peppers, chopped
- 1 tsp. crushed garlic
- Salt and pepper

Directions

1. Stir together tomatoes, onions, cilantro, lemon juice, jalapeno peppers, and garlic.
2. Salt and pepper to taste.
3. Cover and chill 3 hours before serving.

Figure 4-8: *Bulleted lists and numbered lists serve different purposes.*

How to Create a List

Procedure Reference: Create a List from Existing Text

Sometimes a document may already have paragraphs that should be presented in a list. To turn these paragraphs into a list:

1. Select the paragraphs that will be included in the list.
2. Click either the Bullets button or Numbering button on the Formatting toolbar to create the list.

Remove Bullets and Numbering

To remove a bullet or number format from a list item, select the desired paragraph and click the appropriate button on the Formatting toolbar—click the Bullets button to remove a bullet; click the Numbering button to remove a number.

Bullet and Number Formats

You can create a customized list or change a list's bullet or numbering format by selecting the list and choosing Format→Bullets And Numbering. Select the Bulleted tab to see bullet formats and select the Numbered tab to see the various numbering formats. Each tab has additional formatting choices that can be displayed by clicking the Customize button.

Procedure Reference: Create a New List

To create a list from scratch:

1. Place the insertion point where you want to start the list.
2. Select the type of list you want.
   - To create a bulleted list, click the Bullets button on the Formatting toolbar.

     You can also press Ctrl+Shift+L to apply a bullet list.
   - Or, to create a numbered list, click the Numbering button on the Formatting toolbar.
3. Type the first list item and press Enter to move the insertion point to the next line and to start the next list item.
4. After typing the last list item, press Enter twice to end the list. (You can also click the appropriate list button on the Formatting toolbar to end the list.)

Lists and AutoFormat As You Type

When you want to start a new list, you can use Word's AutoFormat As You Type option to automatically start bulleted and numbered lists for you. To start a bulleted list, type an asterisk (*), press Tab, type the list item, and press Enter. Word will convert the asterisk into a bullet and begin a bulleted list for you. To start a numbered list, type the first number of the list and any trailing punctuation, like a period or open parenthesis. Press Tab, type the list item, and press Enter. Again, Word will begin the numbered list using the numbering format you want.

ACTIVITY 4-6

Creating Numbered and Bulleted Lists

Setup:

My Meeting Agenda is open.

Scenario:

The meeting agenda contains some text that would benefit from being formatted as lists. For instance, the three agenda items should show the order of the meeting's events. You also notice that a fourth item, "Assign action items." has been left off the agenda and needs to be added. Also the action items have been decided upon: Tim will distribute the data file; Kris will print the disclaimer inserts; and Ryan will plan the next meeting. These items should be listed below the Action Items heading at the end of the document, though the order doesn't matter.

What You Do	How You Do It
1. Below the "Agenda" heading, **format the three paragraphs as a numbered list.**	a. Below the "Agenda" heading, **select "Review minutes..." through "Approve new disclaimer."**

b. On the Formatting toolbar, **click the Numbering button** to format the selected text as a numbered list, showing the meeting's order of events.

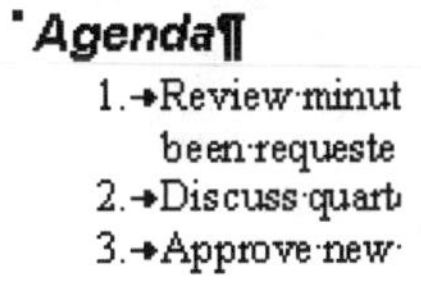
Agenda¶
1.→Review·minut
been·requeste
2.→Discuss·quart
3.→Approve·new·

c. **Deselect the text.**

Notice that Word automatically numbers the items as well as creates a hanging indent.

2. **Add *Assign action items.* as the fourth agenda item.**	a. In the list of agenda items, **place the insertion point at the end of the third item.** 3.→Approve·new·disclaimer.¶ b. **Press Enter** to move the insertion point to the next line and to start a new list item automatically. c. **Type *Assign action items.*** 3.→Approve·new·disclaimer.¶ 4.→Assign·action·items.¶
3. Under the Action Items heading, **create the Action Items bulleted list.** **Action·Items¶** •→Tim·will·distribute·the·data.¶ •→Kris·will·print·the·inserts.¶ •→Ryan·will·plan·the·next·meeting.¶ ¶ ¶	a. At the bottom of the page, **place the insertion point at the end of the "Action Items" heading and press Enter.** b. On the Formatting toolbar, **click the Bullets button** to create a new bulleted list. c. **Type *Tim will distribute the data.* Press Enter.** d. **Type *Kris will print the inserts.* Press Enter.** e. **Type *Ryan will plan the next meeting.* Press Enter.** f. **Press Enter again** to end the bulleted list.

TOPIC G

Change Spacing Between Paragraphs and Lines

Changing paragraph alignment often adds white space around the sides of a paragraph. You can also add white space before, after, and within paragraphs. In this topic, you will learn how to change paragraph spacing.

Which of the following is easier for you to read?

February sales for Tim Jones dipped unexpectedly. His March sales jumped 33%. Missy Lu is By far the best junior sales associate. Her sales were strong despite significant seasonal hurdles. Miles Rodriguez shows steady sales, but seems unmotivated.

February sales for Tim Jones dipped unexpectedly. His March sales jumped 33%.

Missy Lu is By far the best junior sales associate. Her sales were strong despite significant seasonal hurdles.

Miles Rodriguez shows steady sales, but seems unmotivated.

Figure 4-9: *Paragraphs without adequate spacing between them (left) versus paragraphs with adequate spacing.*

A paragraph usually consists of one or more sentences presenting a single idea or topic. By clearly separating paragraphs with additional white space, it's obvious to the reader where one idea ends and another begins. Omitting this white space may cause confusion for the reader, thereby frustrating him or her to the point where he or she will stop reading your text.

How to Change Spacing

Procedure Reference: Change Spacing Between Paragraphs

To change paragraph spacing:

1. Select the paragraph(s) you want to affect.
2. Choose Format→Paragraph.
3. On the Indents And Spacing Tab, under Spacing, use the spin boxes to set the amount of space you want before and/or after a paragraph.

   To remove spacing from before or after a paragraph, set the appropriate spin box to 0.

4. Click OK to apply the spacing changes.

Procedure Reference: Change Line Spacing within Paragraphs

By default, paragraphs contain single-spaced lines of text. To change line spacing:

1. Select the paragraph(s) you want to affect.
2. On the Formatting toolbar, display the Line Spacing button's drop-down list 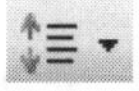 and select the desired amount of line spacing.

You can also change line spacing on the Indents And Spacing Tab in the Paragraph dialog box.

ACTIVITY 4-7

Adding Space Between Paragraphs and Lines of Text

Setup:

My Meeting Agenda is open.

Scenario:

You notice that the text above and below the quarterly sales data is a little close to the borders. You also notice that there isn't enough space between the lines of text in the disclaimer to allow people to write in their comments.

What You Do	How You Do It
1. **Add 6 points of space before the "Houses Sold by Region" table title.**	a. In the quarterly sales data, **place the insertion point in the title, "Houses Sold by Region."**

	b. **Choose Format→Paragraph** to display the Indents And Spacing tab in the Paragraph dialog box.
	c. To add 6 points of spacing before the title, under Spacing, to the right of the Before spin box, **click the up arrow once.**
	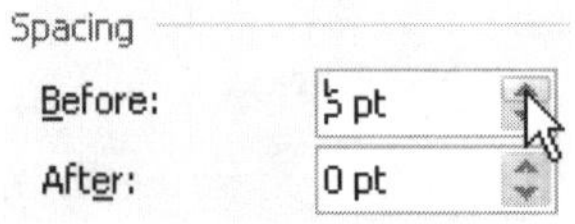
	d. **Click OK.**
2. **Add 6 points of space after the "Source: Burke Properties." paragraph.**	a. **Place the insertion point in the "Source: Burke Properties." paragraph.**

b. In the Paragraph dialog box, to the right of the After spin box, **click the up arrow once** to add 6 points of spacing after the source.

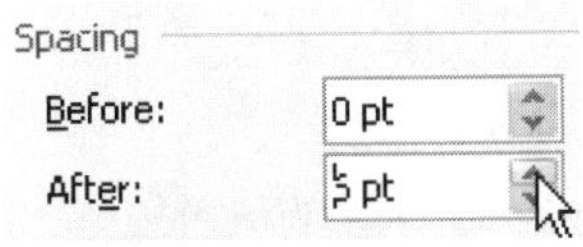

c. **Click OK.**

---

3. To provide space so people can write in their comments, **double-space the disclaimer text.**

a. Inside the shaded disclaimer border, **select all the disclaimer text.**

b. On the Formatting toolbar, **display the Line Spacing button's drop-down list and select 2.0.**

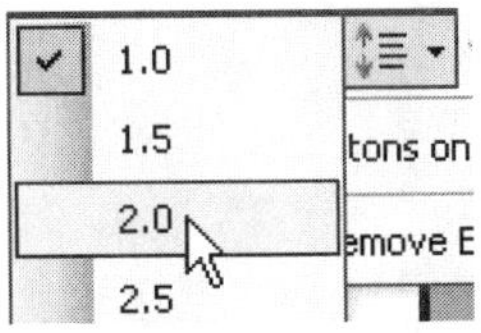

c. **Deselect the text.**

---

4. **Save My Meeting Agenda.**

If you are not going to complete the following practice activity, **close the file.**

PRACTICE ACTIVITY 4-8

Adjusting Space Between Paragraphs and Lines of Text

Scenario:

The disclaimer area needs some more work. The text above the disclaimer title is too close to the border and the lines of text within the disclaimer are too far apart, wasting valuable space. You decide to add space above the disclaimer title and slightly reduce the spacing between the lines—yet still providing room for people to write their comments.

1. **Add 6 points of space above "Disclaimer."**
2. **Reduce line spacing to 1.5 lines.**
3. **Save My Meeting Agenda and close the file.**

Lesson 4 Follow-up

In this lesson, you made a document easier to read and understand by applying various paragraph formatting techniques. To position text where you want it, you used the ruler to set tabs, you used the alignment options to reposition paragraphs horizontally on the page, and you indented paragraphs the way you wanted them. To add visual interest, you added borders and shading to a paragraph. You learned how to apply a style, taking advantage of Word's ability to apply several formats simultaneously. You also enhanced the readability of your document by organizing information in lists and adding space between paragraphs.

1. **What text formatting will you use to enhance the text in your work documents?**
2. **When formatting your work documents, what Word tools will be most advantageous to you and why?**

LESSON 5
Proofing a Document

Lesson Time
40 minutes

Lesson Objectives:

In this lesson, you will use Word tools to make your documents more accurate.

You will:

- Use the Thesaurus to replace words.
- Check spelling and grammar of a document.
- Create a new custom dictionary.
- Check a document's word count.
- Modify a document in Print Preview.

Introduction

Once you are comfortable with the basics of entering text, the next step is to improve your writing. In this lesson, you will use tools that can enhance your writing style as well as automatically correct common typing mistakes.

If your document contains careless errors, the credibility of your message is diminished. You can prevent or correct most writing mistakes using Word's proofing tools.

TOPIC A

Use the Thesaurus

Formatting may emphasize text appearance, but words emphasize your text's meaning. And, as you write, the time may come when you just can't find the word you want to use. In this topic, you will use Word's built-in Thesaurus to help in those situations.

You have written a memo promoting the useful features of your company's new email program. When you asked your co-workers what they thought of the new software, the canned response was, "It's useful." Why did so many people have the same response? You reread the memo and are surprised at how dull it really is. One thing that really stands out is the fact that you described nearly every feature as "useful." So it seems that very few people actually finished reading the memo. If you had a Thesaurus on your desk, you might have avoided this writing rut by trying a wider variety of words, making the memo more readable. Fortunately, with Word, you do have a Thesaurus. And it's just a couple clicks away.

Research Task Pane

The Research task pane lets you look up information using a wide variety of online references. Figure 5-1 shows some of the resources in the Research task pane. To see a complete list of available services, click Research Options at the bottom of the Research task pane.

You can also use the Research task pane to translate text from one language to another.

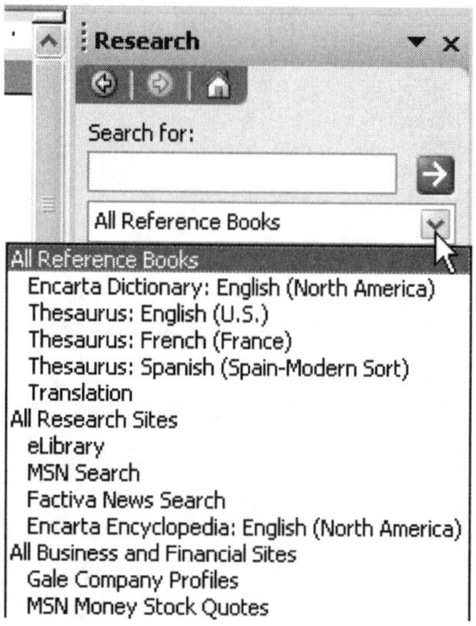

Figure 5-1: *Available research options in the Research task pane.*

To fully utilize the Research task pane, your computer must have an active Internet connection.

Thesaurus

A reference book available in the Research task pane, the *Thesaurus* can be used to look up potential synonyms—words with similar meanings—and antonyms—words with opposite meanings.

How to Use the Thesaurus

Procedure Reference: Use the Thesaurus

To use the Thesaurus:

1. Right-click the word for which you want to find a synonym to display the shortcut menu.
2. Choose Synonyms to display a list of words with similar meanings.

   If a word is misspelled or unrecognized by Word, the Synonyms option will not be available from the shortcut menu.

3. Select the most suitable word to replace the original word.

Procedure Reference: Insert a Synonym from Thesaurus in the Research Task Pane

To insert a synonym from the Research task pane:

1. Right-click the word for which you want to find a synonym.
2. From the shortcut menu, choose Synonyms→Thesaurus to display the Thesaurus in the Research task pane.

   You can also display Thesaurus results in the Research task pane by choosing Tools→Language→Thesaurus, pressing Shift+F7, or pressing Alt and clicking the desired word.

3. Locate the desired synonym.
4. Click the synonym's drop-down list arrow and select Insert to place the word into the document.

ACTIVITY 5-1

Using the Thesaurus to Replace a Word

Data Files:

- Relocation Letter.doc

Setup:

No documents are open.

Scenario:

You've finished writing a relocation letter to a client who will be arriving in Boston soon. You notice that you repeat the word "objective" a few times throughout the letter. After the first time, the word begins to sound trite.

Relocation Letter includes several misspellings and grammatical errors. Do not attempt to correct any of these. You will do so later in this lesson.

What You Do	How You Do It
1. In the second paragraph of the Relocation Letter, **replace the word "objective" with the synonym "goal."**	a. **Open Relocation Letter.** b. In the paragraph that begins with "You will be glad to know...," **right-click the word "objective"** to display the shortcut menu. c. **Choose Synonyms** to display a list of words with similar meanings. d. From the Synonyms submenu, **choose "goal."**
2. In the last paragraph before the closing, **replace the word "objective" with a synonym that means "impartial" from the Thesaurus task pane.**	a. Near the end of the letter, in the sentence that begins with "It is our objective opinion...," **right-click "objective" and display the Synonyms submenu.** b. From the Synonyms submenu, **choose Thesaurus** to display results from the Thesaurus in the Research task pane. c. In the Thesaurus results, **locate synonyms for "impartial (adj.)."**

d. In the Thesaurus results, **place the mouse pointer over "unbiased" and click the drop-down list arrow.** This displays the synonym's options.

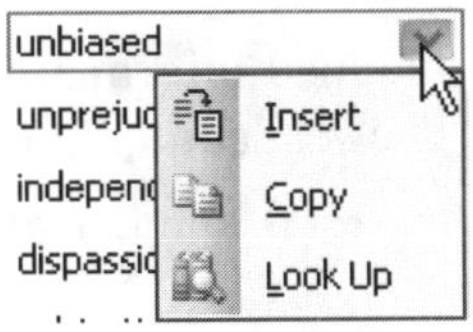

If you accidentally click the word "unbiased," just click the Previous Search, or Back, button.

e. **Select Insert** to insert the word into the document.

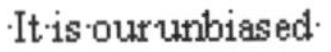

3. **Save the letter as *My Relocation Letter*.**

TOPIC B

Check Spelling and Grammar

Whenever you proofread a document, you should fix spelling and grammar mistakes. Unfortunately, not everyone is good at identifying these errors. In this topic, you will use Word's built-in spelling and grammar tool to help locate and correct errors.

You just found out about a new request for proposal that could bring your company thousands of dollars. The problem is that the deadline is just a few hours away. So you dash off the proposal in Word and email the document, without checking the text for spelling or grammar errors. Though the client liked your ideas, she was appalled by the number of spelling and grammar mistakes in your proposal. Your haste just cost your company a deal. Word's spelling and grammar tool can make your documents more accurate as well as help you to avoid potentially embarrassing mistakes.

Main Dictionary

All programs in the Office System, including Word, use the *main dictionary* to check a document's spelling. As you type or when you run the Spelling And Grammar checker, Word compares your spelling to the list of terms stored in the main dictionary.

The main dictionary does not contain word definitions. The main dictionary is neither editable nor viewable.

Readability Statistics

Word can provide you with detailed information about your documents called *readability statistics*. (See Figure 5-2.) The readability statistics provided are:

- Counts, which include the total number of words, characters, paragraphs, and sentences in the document.
- Averages, the average number of sentences per paragraph, words per sentence, and characters per word.
- And Readability, the percent of passive sentences and readability scores based on the number of syllables per word and the number of words per sentence.

Readability scores are based on the Flesch Reading Ease and the Flesch-Kincaid Grade Level scales. Search Help to find out more about each scale.

Readability Statistics are available only after the option has been enabled and a spell check has been run.

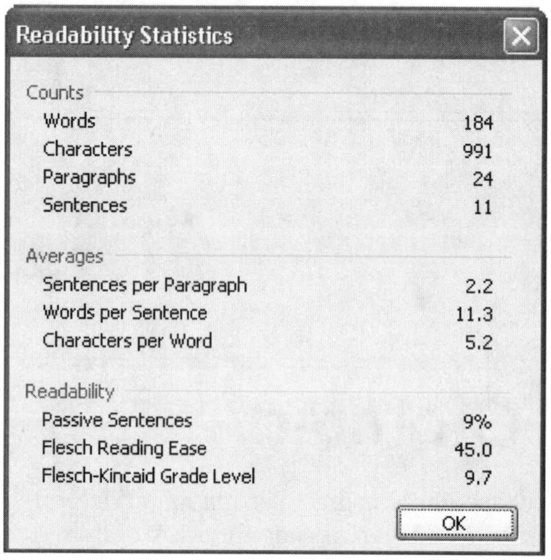

Figure 5-2: *A sample of readability statistics.*

Enable Readability Statistics

Procedure Reference: Enable Readability Statistics

To enable Word's Readability Statistics:

1. Choose Tools→Options.
2. Select the Spelling & Grammar tab.
3. Under Grammar, check the Show Readability Statistics check box.
4. Click OK.

ACTIVITY 5-2

Enabling Readability Statistics

Setup:

My Relocation Letter is open. The Show Readability Statistics option is disabled.

Scenario:

Your manager is interested in maintaining a certain readability level. Before Word can show you that information for a document, the Readability Statistics need to be enabled.

What You Do	How You Do It
1. **Display the Spelling & Grammar tab in the Options dialog box.**	a. **Choose Tools→Options** to display the Options dialog box.
	b. **Select the Spelling & Grammar tab.**
2. **Enable the Readability Statistics.**	a. Under Grammar, **check the Show Readability Statistics check box.**
	b. **Click OK** to enable the option and close the dialog box.

How to Check Spelling and Grammar

Procedure Reference: Check a Misspelled Word or Ungrammatical Sentence

To check a word for spelling or a sentence for grammar:

1. Right-click the misspelled word or ungrammatical sentence to display a list of possible correct options.
2. Choose the correct option to replace the incorrect word or sentence.
3. If you don't see the desired option, use the shortcut menu to display additional options.
   - If it's a spelling error, select Spelling to see more spelling options.
   - Or, if it's a grammar error, select Grammar to see more grammar options.

Procedure Reference: Check Spelling and Grammar in a Document

To check a document's spelling and grammar:

1. Move the insertion point to the top of the document.

   You can also check a specific text selection for spelling and grammar.

2. Display the Spelling And Grammar dialog box.

- On the Standard toolbar, click the Spelling And Grammar button  .
- Choose Tools→Spelling And Grammar.
- Press F7.
- Or, right-click a misspelled word and choose Spelling.

Right-clicking a word or sentence with a wavy underline will display a list of potential corrections and/or explanations of what is wrong with the marked item.

If you click outside the Spelling And Grammar dialog box during a spell check, you will need to click the Resume button in the dialog box to continue checking the text.

3. The first spelling or grammar error is displayed in the Spelling And Grammar dialog box. Indicate how you want to proceed.
    - Click Ignore Once to skip the occurrence this time but find it the next occurrence. In this way, you correct found text on a case-by-case basis.
    - Click Ignore All to leave the highlighted text unchanged and continue searching for the next error.

      If you accidentally ignore an occurrence, you will need to recheck the document. Click Recheck Document on the Spelling And Grammar options tab. The next time you check the document, Word will locate the occurrence you previously ignored.

    - Click Add To Dictionary to add the occurrence to the dictionary. This will allow Word to recognize the occurrence as correct.
    - Click Change to replace the found text with the selected correction from the Suggestions list box.
    - Click AutoCorrect to have Word make the correction for you.
    - Or, click Change All to replace all occurrences of the highlighted text with the suggested word at the same time. Be careful—if you use Change All, you can easily make changes you didn't intend to make.

      If you change your mind after changing text, click the Undo button in the Spelling And Grammar dialog box to return to the last error.

4. Click OK to close either the Spelling And Grammar or Readability Statistics dialog box.

ACTIVITY 5-3

Checking a Document's Spelling and Grammar

Setup:

My Relocation Letter is open and the Readability Statistics option has been enabled.

Scenario:

The letter was typed in a hurry, as several misspellings and grammar problems are indicated by the wavy red and green underlines. You need to review the errors and decide how you want to handle them. Your manager wants you to keep your use of passive sentences below 10 percent

What You Do	How You Do It
1. In the letter's first paragraph, **use the shortcut menu to replace the misspelled word "inquring" and the grammar error.**	a. In the first sentence of the letter, **right-click the misspelled word "inquring"** to display a list of possible correction.
	b. **Select the first option, "inquiring,"** to replace the misspelled word.
	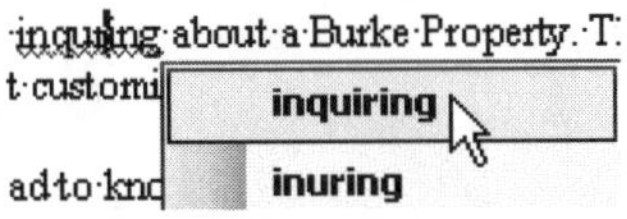
	c. In the second sentence, **right-click in the grammar error** (the text with the wavy green underline).
	d. **Select the first option "Objective Of Burke Properties Is"** to correct the ungrammatical text.

2. With the insertion point at the top of the document, **display the Spelling And Grammar dialog box.**

   a. **Move the insertion point to the top of the letter.**

   b. On the Standard toolbar, **click the Spelling And Grammar button** .

---

3. **Correct obvious mistakes and ignore those that you may be unsure about, such as "TeamServe," "Beantown," and "BurkeBuddy."**

   Do not click Ignore All when a term isn't recognized by the Spelling And Grammar tool.

   a. Word stops on the misspelled word "complament." Since the correct spelling, "complement," is already selected in the Suggestions list box, **click Change** to correct the spelling and continue.

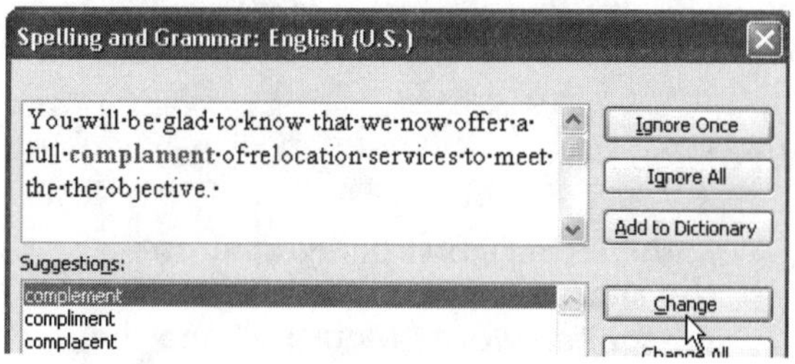

   b. Word found the word "the" has been repeated. **Click Delete.**

   c. The word "TeamServe" isn't recognized, but it's correct. **Click Ignore Once** to skip this occurrence.

   d. The word "Beantown" isn't recognized, but it's correct. **Click Ignore Once** to skip this occurrence.

   e. The word "BurkeBuddy" isn't recognized, but it too is correct. **Click Ignore Once.**

   f. A capitalization error is found. **Click Change** to fix the error.

   g. A Subject-Verb Agreement grammar problem is found. **Click Change.**

---

4. **What is the percentage of passive sentences in the document?**___

---

5. **Click OK** to close the Readability Statistics dialog box.

TOPIC C

Create a New Default Dictionary

When you spell check a document, Word may incorrectly mark non-standard words as errors—even if they are technically correct. If these words were added to a new default dictionary they wouldn't show up as errors. In this topic, you will create a new default dictionary containing words common to your documents.

You are spell-checking your product catalog and Word is pausing on terms such as AceGrip, PowerHold, and TightLock—perfectly correct names for unique products that you sell. Unfortunately, Word doesn't know that. And because the catalog document contains hundreds of such product names, the spell check will take much longer than it should. You could ignore all occurrences, but the next time you spell check a different document that contains those terms, the same thing will happen. Rather than repeatedly ignoring the terms, you can tell Word that these terms are correct. Once you do that, Word will ignore the terms if they are correctly spelled, but it will still catch the misspelled ones. This will speed up your spell checks as well as improve its accuracy.

Custom Dictionaries

When you perform a spell check, Word looks up each word using the main dictionary. If a word isn't found there, Word automatically accesses supplemental, or custom, dictionaries. A *custom dictionary* is a list of words that you provide, such as names and business jargon. Once added to a custom dictionary, Word will ignore the term during a spell-check and as you type it. By default, Word includes one custom dictionary, Custom.dic. However, you can create or import other custom dictionaries as needed.

Like the main dictionary, custom dictionaries are used by all Office System programs.

How to Create a New Default Dictionary

Procedure Reference: Create a New Default Dictionary

To create a new default dictionary:

1. Choose Tools→Options and select the Spelling & Grammar tab.
2. Click Custom Dictionaries to display the Custom Dictionaries dialog box.
3. Click New to display the Create Custom Dictionary dialog box.
4. Name the new custom dictionary and click Save.
5. Select the new dictionary in the Dictionary List box and click Change Default. The new dictionary is made the default dictionary, displayed in bold, and moved to the top of the list.
6. Click OK.

Procedure Reference: Add Words to the Default Dictionary

To add words to the default dictionary while spell-checking a document:

1. Begin spell-checking a document containing words that you want to add.

As you type, if a correct word is flagged with a wavy red underline, you can quickly add it to the default dictionary by right-clicking the word and selecting Add To Dictionary from the shortcut menu.

2. When an unrecognized word is found that you want to include in the default dictionary, click Add To Dictionary.
3. Continue adding words as needed.

Procedure Reference: Modify a Dictionary

You can see words listed, add words to, and delete words from any dictionary at any time by using Modify to display a dictionary. To modify a dictionary:

1. Choose Tools→Options and select the Spelling & Grammar tab.
2. Click Custom Dictionaries to display the Custom Dictionaries dialog box.
3. Select the dictionary to which you want to add or delete terms.
4. Click Modify to display the list of words included in the dictionary.
   - To add a word to the dictionary, type the desired word and click Add, repeating as needed.
   - Or, to delete a word from the dictionary, select the desired word in the Dictionary list box and click Delete, repeating as needed.
5. Click OK twice.

Managing Dictionaries

Once a dictionary has been created, you can choose whether or not Word uses it by checking or unchecking the dictionary in the Dictionary list box. From the list, you can also remove a dictionary by selecting it and clicking Remove. This just takes the dictionary off the list; it doesn't delete the dictionary. To do that, click either New or Add. In the subsequent dialog box you can select the desired dictionary and press Delete. Click Yes to confirm the deletion.

ACTIVITY 5-4

Creating a New Custom Dictionary

Data Files:

- Relocation Listing.doc

Setup:

My Relocation Letter is open.

Scenario:

The relocation listing needs to be spell-checked too. It contains many of the product names you just ignored while spell-checking the relocation letter. Rather than ignore the names again, you decide to create a new default, Product Names dictionary to add the desired words.

What You Do	How You Do It
1. With the relocation listing document open, **display the Custom Dictionaries dialog box.**	a. **Open Relocation Listing.** b. **Choose Tools→Options.** c. On the Spelling & Grammar tab, under Spelling, **click Custom Dictionaries.**
2. **What is the name of the current default dictionary?**__________	
3. **Create a new dictionary named *Product Names.dic*.**	a. **Click New** to display the Create Custom Dictionary dialog box. b. In the File Name drop-down list box, **type *Product Names*** c. **Click Save.** ⚠ If Word prompts you that the file Product Names.dic already exists, click Yes to replace it.

4. **Set the Product Names dictionary as the default dictionary.**

   a. In the Dictionary List box, **select Product Names.dic.**

   Be careful not to uncheck the Product Names.dic file.

   b. **Click Change Default.**

   The Product Names dictionary is bold with the word default in parentheses, and the new dictionary moves to the top of the list.

   c. **Click OK** to close the Custom Dictionaries dialog box.

   d. **Click OK** to close the Options dialog box.

---

5. **Spell check the relocation listing, adding "Beantown," "TeamServe," and "BurkeBuddy" to the Product Listing dictionary.**

   a. On the Standard toolbar, **click the Spelling And Grammar button** to begin the spell check.

   b. As expected, Word doesn't recognize "Beantown." **Click Add To Dictionary** to add it to the Product Names dictionary and continue the spell check.

   c. **Add both "TeamServe" and "BurkeBuddy" to the dictionary.**

   d. **Click OK** to close the Readability Statistics dialog box.

---

6. **Display the Product Names dictionary.**

   a. **Display the Options dialog box.**

   b. On the Spelling & Grammar tab, **click Custom Dictionaries.**

   c. With Product Names.dic, selected **click Modify** to display the list of words included in the dictionary.

---

7. **True or False? "Beantown," "BurkeBuddy," and "TeamServe" are listed in the Product Names.dic.**

   __ True

   __ False

---

8. **Add the *SoldByBurke* word** to the Product Names dictionary.

   a. In the Word text box, **type *SoldByBurke***

b. **Click Add.**

c. **Click OK** to close the Product Names dictionary.

d. **Click OK** to close the Custom Dictionaries dialog box.

e. **Click OK** to close the Options dialog box.

TOPIC D

Check Word Count

A document you are writing must be a specific number of words. You needn't count the words yourself. In this topic, you will use the Word Count tool to help you determine how many words are in a document.

You are writing a column for the company newsletter. The column has a 400-word limit. After half an hour, you're really rolling, the ideas are flowing, but you have to break the momentum to stop and count how many words you have typed so far. You could spell check the document to see a word count displayed in the Readability Statistics, but you're not ready to spell check the article yet. So you start counting, when the phone rings and you lose your place. You start counting over again. After counting about 350 words, your mind starts to wander. When you've finished, you're not sure if you have 395 or 405 words. You submit the column, relying on your editor to get it to fit. The editor responds, "Nice article. However, because it's 450 words, it needs too much work. Thanks anyway." If you only had a quick and accurate way to determine word count whenever you want it. With Word, you do.

How to Check Word Counts

Procedure Reference: Use Word Count

To count the number of words:

1. Indicate the text that is to be counted.

- If you want to count the number of words in a specific piece of text, select it.
- Or, if you want to count the number of words in the entire document, do not select any text.

2. Choose Tools→Word Count. The Word Count dialog box displays the counted statistics.

Press Ctrl+Shift+G to display the Word Count dialog box.

3. Click Cancel.

Word Count Toolbar

If you want to make it easy to keep a running count, display the Word Count toolbar. (Choose View→Toolbars→Word Count or click Show Toolbar in the Word Count dialog box.) Just click the Recount button as often as you want to see a refreshed count at any time. Display the Word Count Statistics drop-down list to see character, line, page, and paragraph counts too.

ACTIVITY 5-5

Counting Words in a Document

Setup:

Relocation Listing is open.

Scenario:

You have almost completed the relocation listing. It must be 275 words or less to fit in the mailing going out next week. If you need to, you can cut text from the unhighlighted part of the guarantee. It essentially repeats what will be stated in the letter that accompanies the list.

What You Do | **How You Do It**

1. **Count how many words are in the Relocation Listing document and display the Word Count toolbar.**

   a. With no text selected, **choose Tools→ Word Count.**

   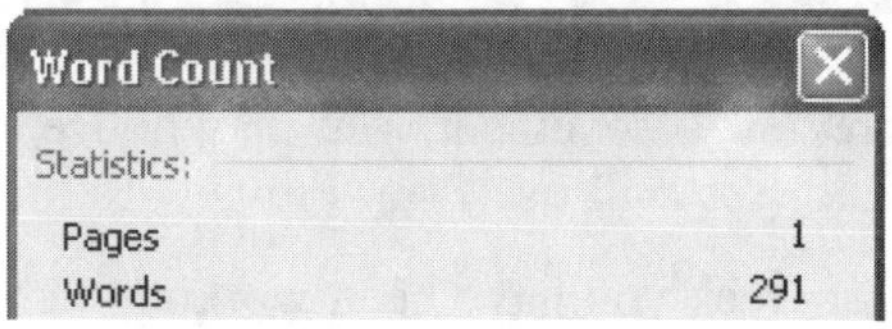

   b. The document contains 291 words. **Click Show Toolbar** to display the Word Count toolbar.

   c. In the Word Count dialog box, **click Close.**

2. After the "Our Guarantee:" inline heading, **select and count the number of words in the unhighlighted text.**

   a. In the last paragraph, **select "We are so sure...real estate needs, that" and the following space.**

   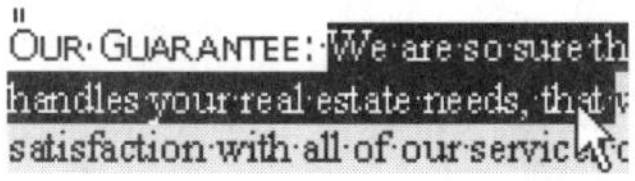

   b. On the Word Count toolbar, **click Recount** to count the number of words in the selection.

3. **How many words are in the selection?**___

4. **Delete the selected text and recount the number of words in the document. (Don't forget to capitalize the "w" in "we unconditionally guarantee....")**

   a. With "We are so sure...real estate needs, that" and the following space selected, **press Delete and capitalize the "w" in "we."**

   You may need to highlight the "W."

   b. On the Word Count toolbar, **click Recount.**

5. **How many words are in the document after the deletion?**___

6. The document now meets the 275-word limit. **Close the Word Count toolbar.**

   Save the document as *My Relocation Listing* and close it.

TOPIC E

Modify a Document in Print Preview

As you preview a document, you may notice some last-minute changes that need to be made. In this topic, you will use Print Preview to modify a document.

For the last week you have been working on a business proposal for a potential client. One of the stipulations of the proposal is that it cannot exceed five pages. If the proposal exceeds that limit, it will not be considered—your efforts will be wasted. You preview the document and it's exactly five pages long. Your manager then asks you to insert a one-paragraph legal disclaimer, which pushes the document over the limit. You need to meet the proposal's requirements as well as your manager's request without sacrificing meaningful text. Word can help you accomplish both.

How to Modify a Document in Print Preview

Procedure Reference: Edit a Document in Print Preview

To edit your document in Print Preview:

1. Display the document in Print Preview.
2. If necessary, display the page you want to edit.
3. Use the Magnifier to zoom in on the area you want to edit.
4. Click the Magnifier button  on the Print Preview toolbar to change the mouse pointer from a magnifying glass to an I-beam.
5. Edit the document.
6. Click the Magnifier or close Print Preview to restore the tool.

Procedure Reference: Fit a Document on a Page

To keep a document from spilling over to an extra page:

1. In Print Preview, click the Shrink To Fit button  .

Undo Shrink To Fit

When you click Shrink To Fit in Print Preview, Word reduces the font size of all the text in the document to reduce the document's total page count. You may not want to keep these changes. If that's the case, before you save and close the document, be sure to choose Edit→Undo Shrink To Fit to restore the original font settings.

ACTIVITY 5-6

Modifying a Document in Print Preview

Setup:

My Relocation Listing and the Word Count toolbar are closed. My Relocation Letter is displayed.

Scenario:

You are determined to finish the letter and prepare it for printing. As you preview the document, you notice that the letter is longer than one page. You want to make it fit on one sheet of paper when printed. You also see a couple of edits that need to be made, such as adding the date and finishing your job title, "Relocation Specialist," in the letter's closing.

What You Do	How You Do It
1. **Preview the letter using the full screen.**	a. On the Standard toolbar, **click the Print Preview button** .
	b. On the Print Preview toolbar, **click the Full Screen button** to hide title, menu, and scroll bars, viewing as much of the document as possible.
2. At the top of the page, **edit the document by typing today's date on the blank line below Seattle.**	a. With the Magnifier, **zoom in on the top of the page.**
	b. On the Print Preview toolbar, **click the Magnifier button** to edit the document.
	c. **Place the insertion point on the line below the city, state, and Zip code.** Ms. Marcy York Tangent Allied Services 2802 SW Barton St. Seattle, WA 98126
	d. **Type today's date.** AutoComplete even works in Print Preview.

3. Near the bottom of the page, **complete the job title by typing *Specialist*.**

   a. On the Full Screen toolbar, **click Close Full Screen** to redisplay the vertical scroll bar in Print Preview.

   b. **Display the bottom of the first page.**

   c. On the line below the name, **place the insertion point after "Relocation."**

   Tim Jones
   Relocation
   Burke Properties, Inc.

   d. **Press the Spacebar once and type *Specialist***

---

4. Since the document is just a few lines over, **shrink the document so that it fits on one page then close the Preview.**

   a. On the Print Preview toolbar, **click the Shrink To Fit button**. The document now fits neatly on one page.

   b. On the Print Preview toolbar, **click Close** to redisplay the document in Print Layout view.

---

5. **What's the font size of all the text in the document?**__

---

6. **Why isn't the text 12 pt?**

---

7. **Save and close My Relocation Letter.**

Lesson 5 Follow-up

In this lesson, you used several proofing tools to make your documents more accurate. You used the Thesaurus to locate just the right word. You corrected a document's spelling and grammar errors. You created a custom dictionary to make the spell checker more accurate. You used Word Count to help you keep track of a document's length. And lastly, you made minor changes to a document in Print Preview. When combined, these tools can have quite a positive effect on your documents and how you create them day to day.

1. **Of all of the proofing tools used in this lesson, which one do you think will help you create more accurate documents?**

2. **Based on what you learned in this lesson, how do you think these proofing tools will impact the way you proof documents?**

Notes

LESSON 6
Adding Tables

Lesson Time
40 minutes

Lesson Objectives:

In this lesson, you will add tables to a document.

You will:

- Create a table.
- Enter information in a table.
- AutoFormat a table.
- Convert text into a table.

Introduction

To this point, you've been primarily focused on entering and modifying text. That's important, but so is how that text is arranged and presented on the page. In this lesson, you will discover how conveniently tables can be used to organize and enhance information.

Sometimes when data is presented as a list or a paragraph, it can be difficult for readers to process. When you use tables appropriately, they can significantly improve reader comprehension by enabling you to organize your information and eliminate unnecessary words.

TOPIC A

Create a Table

Entering information in a document is one thing. Arranging it in the most readable format is another. In this topic, you will create a new table to help you organize information.

Presenting textual information is what word processing is all about. But when that text contains data, often the data gets buried, making it difficult to read. (See Figure 6-1.) Usually, the reader will benefit from seeing the data arranged in columns and rows. You may try aligning the data in a table-like format using the Spacebar or inserting tabs, perhaps producing reasonable results, but if you ever need to change the data or how it's formatted, you will likely have problems. By far, the most effective and efficient way to present data in columns and rows is to use tables. In short, tables make information more readily accessible to the reader with the least amount of effort by you.

Here's the monthly data for the number of houses sold by the Junior Sales Associates. In January, Tim Jones sold 71 houses, then 66 in February, and 99 in March. Missy Lu sold 155 houses in January, 164 in February, and 213 in March. Miles Rodriguez sold 130 houses in January, 132 in February, and 140 in March. In total, the Junior Sales Associates sold 356 houses in January, 362 in February, and 452 in March. Everyone did much better in March!

Jr. Sales Associate	**Jan**	**Feb**	**Mar**
Tim Jones	71	66	99
Missy Lu	155	164	213
Miles Rodriguez	130	132	140
Total	*356*	*362*	*452*

Figure 6-1: *Similar information presented in a paragraph (left) and in a table (right).*

Tables

A table is a container used to organize text, data, or pictures. Tables consist of boxes called cells. A group of cells arranged vertically is called a column. A group of cells arranged horizontally is called a row. (See Figure 6-2.)

By default, Word applies a thin black border to the entire table.

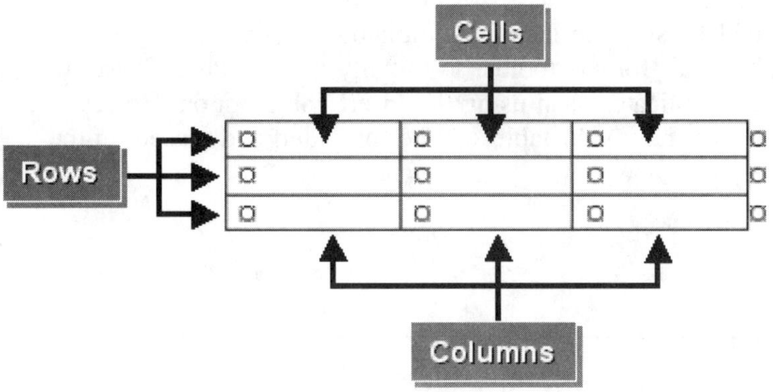

Figure 6-2: *Typical table elements.*

Non-printing Characters in Tables

When non-printing characters are displayed, a table shows several non-printing characters. Each cell contains an end-of-cell marker to indicate the end of each cell. To the right of each row is an end-of-row marker that indicates the end of the row. A column marker appears in the ruler at the boundary of each column. You can use these markers to select table elements. In addition to these markers, Word also displays non-printing gridlines around the table cells. If a table has borders applied to it, gridlines are beneath the borders. To show or hide gridlines on the screen, you choose Table→ Hide Gridlines. (See Figure 6-3.)

Gridlines are sometimes called boundaries.

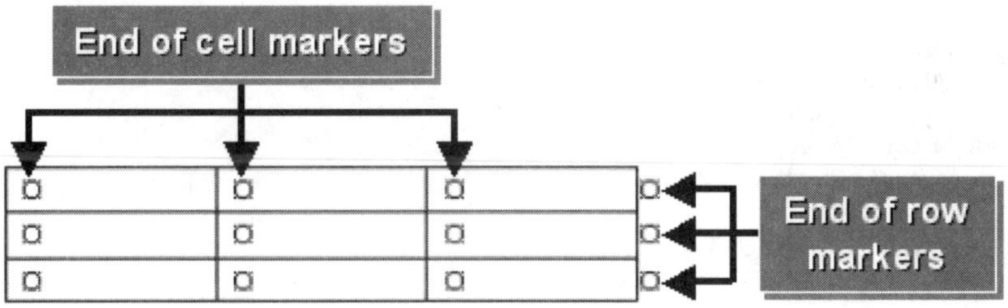

Figure 6-3: *Non-printing characters in a table.*

How to Create a Table

Procedure Reference: Create a Table Using the Insert Table Button

To create a new table using the Insert Table button:

1. Place the insertion point where you want to insert the table.
2. On the Standard toolbar, click the Insert Table button  to display the table size grid.
3. In the grid, click and drag to select the desired number of rows and columns.

   Each cell in the grid represents one cell in the table.

4. Release the mouse button to insert the new table into the document.

Other Table Creation Methods

You can also create new tables using the Insert Table dialog box (choose Table→Insert→Table) or the Tables And Borders toolbar to literally draw a table. These two methods are slightly more complicated than using the Insert Table button. However, they do offer more control over how your table will be formatted and placed on the page.

ACTIVITY 6-1

Inserting a Table

Data Files:

- Sales Data.doc

Setup:

No documents are open.

Scenario:

Your manager has supplied you with a document named Sales Data. (See Figure 6-4.) The data is rather difficult to follow in paragraph form. You decide that the data would work better in a table, with a row for each salesperson and the totals and a column for each month of data.

Here's the monthly data for the number of houses sold by the Junior Sales Associates. In January, Tim Jones sold 71 houses, then 66 in February, and 99 in March. Missy Lu sold 155 houses in January, 164 in February, and 213 in March. Miles Rodriguez sold 130 houses in January, 132 in February, and 140 in March. In total, the Junior Sales Associates sold 356 houses in January, 362 in February, and 452 in March. Everyone did much better in March!

Figure 6-4: *Text from your manager.*

What You Do	How You Do It
1. **Based upon the text provided by your manager, how many rows will you include in the table?_**	
2. **Based upon the text provided by your manager, how many columns will you include in the table?_**	

3. **Insert a new table with five rows and four columns at the bottom of the Sales Data document.**

a. **Open Sales Data.**

b. **Move the insertion point to the end of the document.**

c. On the Standard toolbar, **click the Insert Table button** to display the table size grid.

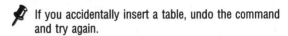

d. In the table size grid, **place the mouse pointer over the first cell.**

e. **Press the mouse button and drag straight down to select five rows and continue dragging to the right to select four columns.**

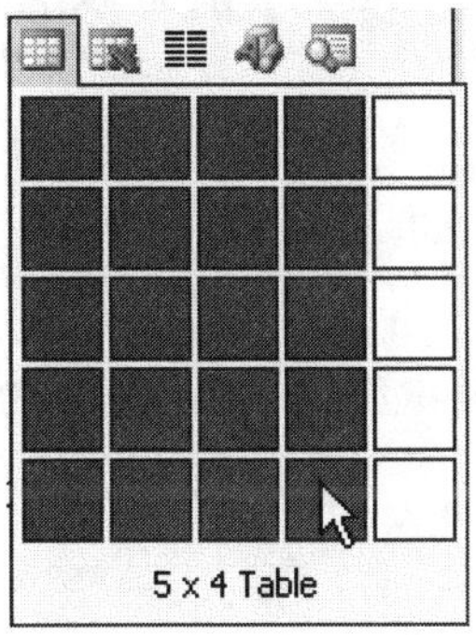

You must press and drag in the table size grid to get the grid to expand beyond four rows. If you are only moving the insertion point over the grid without pressing the mouse button, you will be limited to only four rows.

If you accidentally insert a table, undo the command and try again.

f. **Release the mouse button** to insert the 5 x 4 table into the document.

---

4. **Where is the insertion point?**
   a) Before the table.
   b) After the table.
   c) In the first cell of the table.
   d) In the last cell of the table.
   e) At the top of the document.

---

5. **Which non-printing characters are displayed in the table?**

    a) End-of-row markers.

    b) End-of-cell markers.

    c) End-of-column markers.

    d) End-of-table markers.

6. **Save the document as *My Sales Data*.**

TOPIC B

Enter Data in a Table

With the knowledge of how to create a table, you are now ready to fill it with information. In this topic, you will enter data in your own table.

If you try to create a table-like structure using tabs, you are constantly dividing your attention between positioning tab stops and entering the information. And you may have to reposition all the tab stops just to keep the information aligned. In contrast, because a table's columns automatically keep information aligned, you can concentrate on just entering the information in the table. This can help reduce data entry errors while maintaining the appearance of your data.

Move Around in a Table

Moving the insertion point between cells in a table is critical to entering information in a table effectively. You can move the insertion point in a table by clicking in the desired cell, but this requires you to use the mouse, which can slow you down when you're entering information. Using the keyboard will help you move around quicker in a table. Table 6-1 displays some basic table navigation techniques. It's worth mentioning that some keyboard navigation techniques that you learned for moving the insertion point in the text area may work differently within a table, such as the Tab key.

Table 6-1: *Using the Keyboard to Move Around in a Table*

To Move	Press
One cell to the right	Tab or Right Arrow
One cell to the left	Shift+Tab or Left Arrow
Down one row	Down Arrow
Up one row	Up Arrow

Add a Row to the Bottom of a Table

As you use the keyboard to navigate in a table, it is possible to inadvertently add a new row to the bottom of the table. (Pressing Tab when the insertion point is located in the last cell will add a new row.) If you don't want the extra row, simply undo the action.

DISCOVERY ACTIVITY 6-2

Navigating in a Table

Setup:

My Sales Data is open.

Scenario:

You want to be able to enter information in a table in the most efficient manner possible, so you decide to take a minute to practice moving the insertion point around in the table that you just created.

---

1. **Move the insertion point around the table.** Use the keyboard techniques listed in Table 6-1 as a guide.

   ⚠ If you inadvertently change the table, such as adding a new row to the table, close the file and reopen it.

How to Enter Data in a Table

Procedure Reference: Enter Data in a Table

To type information in a table:

1. Place the insertion point in the appropriate cell.
2. Type the desired information.
3. Navigate to the next cell.
4. Repeat as needed.

Add a Tab to a Cell

Like when adding information to the text area, within a table cell you can start new paragraphs (press Enter) or break a line (press Shift+Enter). However, adding a tab to a cell is different because pressing Tab will move the insertion point to the next cell. To insert a tab within a cell, press Ctrl+Tab.

Type Text Before a Table

When a table is at the beginning of a document, there's no obvious way to type text above the table. The trick is to place the insertion point in the first cell of the first row and press Enter. You can then type as much text as you want.

ACTIVITY 6-3

Typing Information in a Table

Setup:

My Sales Data is open.

Scenario:

With the table created, you are ready to begin entering the sales data. Figure 6-5 shows what the table should look like at the end of this activity.

Jr. Sales Associate¤	Jan¤	Feb¤	Mar¤	¤
Tim Jones¤	71¤	66¤	99¤	¤
¤	¤	¤	¤	¤
¤	¤	¤	¤	¤
¤	¤	¤	¤	¤

Figure 6-5: *Completed data for the first junior sales associate.*

What You Do	How You Do It
1. At the top of the table, **type the table headings: *Associate, Jan, Feb, Mar*.**	a. In the first row, **place the insertion point in the first cell.**
	b. **Type *Associate***
	c. **Press Tab** to move the insertion point one cell to the right.
	You can also use the Right Arrow key to move the insertion point to the right.
	d. **Type *Jan***
	e. **Press Tab** to move the insertion point one cell to the right.
	f. **Type *Feb***
	g. **Press Tab** to move the insertion point one cell to the right.
	h. **Type *Mar***
2. **Edit the Associate heading so that it reads *Jr. Sales Associate*.**	a. To select the "Associate" cell, **press Shift+Tab three times.**
	b. **Type *Jr. Sales Associate*** to replace the old heading with the new one.

3. In the second row, **type the sales data for Tim Jones.** See Figure 6-5 for details.

   a. **Press the Down Arrow once** to move the insertion point to the first cell in the second row.

   b. **Type *Tim Jones***

   c. **Press Tab and type *71*** as his January sales figure.

   d. **Press Tab and type *66*** as his February sales figure.

   e. **Press Tab and type *99*** as his March sales figure.

PRACTICE ACTIVITY 6-4

Completing the Table

Scenario:

You need to finish typing the remaining data into the table. Figure 6-6 shows the completed table.

Jr. Sales Associate	Jan	Feb	Mar
Tim Jones	71	66	99
Missy Lu	155	164	213
Miles Rodriguez	130	132	140
Total	356	362	452

Figure 6-6: *All sales data for January, February, and March.*

1. **Finish typing the data into the table for the other two junior sales associates as well as the monthly totals.** Use Figure 6-6 as your guide.

TOPIC C

AutoFormat a Table

With your data now entered properly in a basic table, it's a good time to enhance the table. In this topic, you will quickly format a table, applying a variety of formatting options all at once.

Just because information is presented in a table, doesn't mean that it looks as good as it could. The right combination of formats can make the information really stand out. You already know how many steps can be involved in formatting text. Tables are no different; you have a wide variety of fonts, font styles, effects, borders, and shading options from which to choose. But rather than spending a lot of time trying to find just the right look, Word enables you to select from an existing set of pre-formatted table designs and apply them automatically to your table. This lets you experiment with a wider variety of formatting choices much more quickly.

How to AutoFormat a Table

Procedure Reference: Automatically Format a Table

To apply a pre-formatted table design to an existing table:

1. Place the insertion point in the table that you want to format.
2. Display the Table AutoFormat dialog box.
   - Choose Table→Table AutoFormat.
   - Or, click the Table AutoFormat button  on the Tables And Borders toolbar.
3. In the Table AutoFormat dialog box, make a selection in the Table Styles list box.
4. Click Apply to apply the formatting to the table.

ACTIVITY 6-5

AutoFormatting a Table

Setup:

My Sales Data is open and the previous practice activity has been completed.

Scenario:

With all the necessary information entered into the table, you notice that it looks kind of dull and the totals don't stand out as much as you want. You really want to draw attention to the March totals, as everyone showed improvement in that month. The only problem is that you don't have much time to devote to formatting the table.

What You Do	How You Do It
1. **Using text formatting techniques, how might you make the table text more readable?**	
2. **Display the Table AutoFormat dialog box.**	a. **Place the insertion point in the table.** b. **Choose Table→Table AutoFormat.** The default Table AutoFormat is Table Grid.
3. **Preview several different Table styles.**	a. In the Table AutoFormat dialog box, in the Table Styles list box, **select various table styles.**
4. **What kind of formatting do you notice being applied to the text and table in the Preview area?**	
5. **Apply Table Grid 8** to the table.	a. In the Table Styles list box, **select Table Grid 8.** b. **Click Apply** to apply the table AutoFormat and to close the dialog box. c. **Save and close My Sales Data.**

TOPIC D

Convert Text into a Table

Creating a new table from scratch is a lot of work, especially if the data is already in the document and you have to retype it in a table. In this topic, you will convert existing tabbed-text into a new table.

You've been asked to update the new product catalog sheet. The person who originally created the document in Word didn't know how to create a table so he used tabs instead. Unfortunately, he didn't know how to set tab stops either—the document is a mess. The information would certainly be more readable if it were put into a formatted table. But since it's several pages, it would take a long time to retype and format all the information in a new table, not to mention you may make mistakes as you type. Mercifully, Word can quickly convert the existing tabbed text into a table, without the risk of mistakes, and you can AutoFormat the table at the same time, too.

How to Convert Tabbed Text into a Table

Procedure Reference: Convert Tabbed Text into an Unformatted Table

To convert tabbed text into an unformatted table:

1. Select the tabbed text that you want to convert into a table.

   It's helpful to have non-printing characters displayed so you can see the tabs. (Click the Show/Hide button.)

   Extra tabs in the text will be converted into empty cells when the table is created.

2. Click the Insert Table button on the Standard toolbar.

Procedure Reference: Convert Tabbed Text into a Formatted Table

To convert tabbed text into a new formatted table:

1. Select the tabbed text that you want to convert into a table.
2. Choose Table→Convert→Text To Table.
3. In the Convert Text To Table dialog box, select the desired settings.
   - To set the table size, select the number of columns.
   - To make the table fit the text, select AutoFit To Contents.
   - To apply a table AutoFormat, click AutoFormat.

- Or, to determine where the columns will be inserted in the text, select a Separate Text At option.

4. Click OK to convert the tabbed text into a new table.

> You can convert a table back into tabbed text by selecting the table and choosing Table→Convert→Table To Text.

Convert Text To Table Options

You can make some other decisions in the Convert Text To Table dialog box. For instance, you can choose the number of columns the new table will have, as well as how wide the columns will be by adjusting the AutoFit behavior options. Word can also convert comma-separated text into tables too. (Comma-separated data is a common data format used by both government and industry.)

ACTIVITY 6-6

Converting Existing Tabbed Text into New Tables

Data Files:

- Burke Review.doc

Scenario:

Your co-worker has asked you to help her with the Burke Review document. She's having trouble using tabs to present the text the way she wants.

What You Do / **How You Do It**

1. In the Burke Review document, **convert the first block of tabbed text into a basic table.**

Tim Jones	His February sales dipped unexpectedly. However he showed a 33% jump in March. Recommend continued mentoring with a senior associate.
Missy Lu	By far the best junior sales associate. Her sales were increasingly strong despite seasonal hurdles. Recommend promotion at first opportunity.
Miles Rodriguez	Shows steady sales, but seems unmotivated. Recommend testing the new incentive programs on him to see if that translates into sales.

a. **Open Burke Review**

b. **Select the tabbed text, "Tim Jones..." through "...translates into sales."**

c. On the Standard toolbar, **click the Insert Table button** .

d. **Deselect the table.**

2. **Convert the second block of tabbed data into a table that fits the contents exactly and has the Table Professional table style applied.**

Jr. Sales Associate	Jan	Feb	Mar
Tim Jones	71	66	99
Missy Lu	155	164	213
Miles Rodriguez	130	132	140

a. At the bottom of the document, **select the tabbed data, "Jr. Sales Associate..." through "...140."**

b. **Choose Table→Convert→Text To Table** to display the Convert Text To Table dialog box.

Based on the tabs in the selected text, Word automatically assumes you want to have four columns in the table.

c. Under AutoFit Behavior, **select the AutoFit To Contents option.**

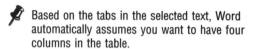

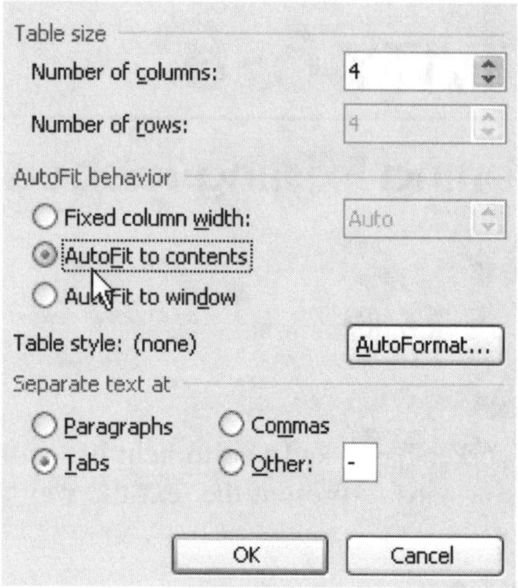

d. **Click AutoFormat** to display the Table AutoFormat dialog box.

e. In the Table Styles list box, **select Table Professional and click OK.**

f. **Click OK** to convert the tabbed text into a formatted table.

g. **Deselect the table.**

3. **Save the document as *My Burke Review* and close it.**

Lesson 6 Follow-up

In this lesson, you learned how to present new and existing information in a table. You successfully created a table and then entered and formatted the data. Lastly, you converted existing tabbed-text into its own table, making it easier to format. Keep in mind that sometimes when data is presented as a list or a paragraph, it can be difficult for readers to process. So use tables whenever possible, as they can significantly improve reader comprehension by enabling you to organize your information more clearly.

1. **How will you use tables in your documents?**

2. **What type of information will you put in tables?**

Notes

LESSON 7
Inserting Graphic Elements

Lesson Time
30 minutes

Lesson Objectives:

In this lesson, you will add graphic elements to a document.

You will:

- Insert a symbol and special character.
- Insert a clip art picture.
- Add a watermark.

Introduction

So far, you have been working with text-based documents. In this lesson, you will gain some hands-on experience adding graphic elements to a document.

We're bombarded with documents every day. Many of them go unread, because, at first glance, there is nothing special about how they look. When you include graphic elements in a document, you increase the likelihood that people will read and remember the document and its message.

TOPIC A

Insert Symbols and Special Characters

Graphic elements certainly add visual interest to documents, but in many cases they can also add meaning. Symbols and special characters are good examples of this. In this topic, you will insert symbols and special characters.

You are drafting a copyright statement and the new department style guide requires that you use the copyright symbol, ©, along with the word "copyright." You've stared at your keyboard for several minutes trying to locate the character, but it's no where to be found. How are you going to get the circle around the letter "c"? You know it can be done, but how? Word provides convenient access to a large group of symbols and special characters, such as the copyright character, that can be inserted quickly and correctly.

Symbols

Symbols are text characters that are not readily available on the standard keyboard, such as accent marks for foreign languages or currency symbols. Each font may have a slightly different set of symbols. You can use the Symbol dialog box to review them. (See Figure 7-1.)

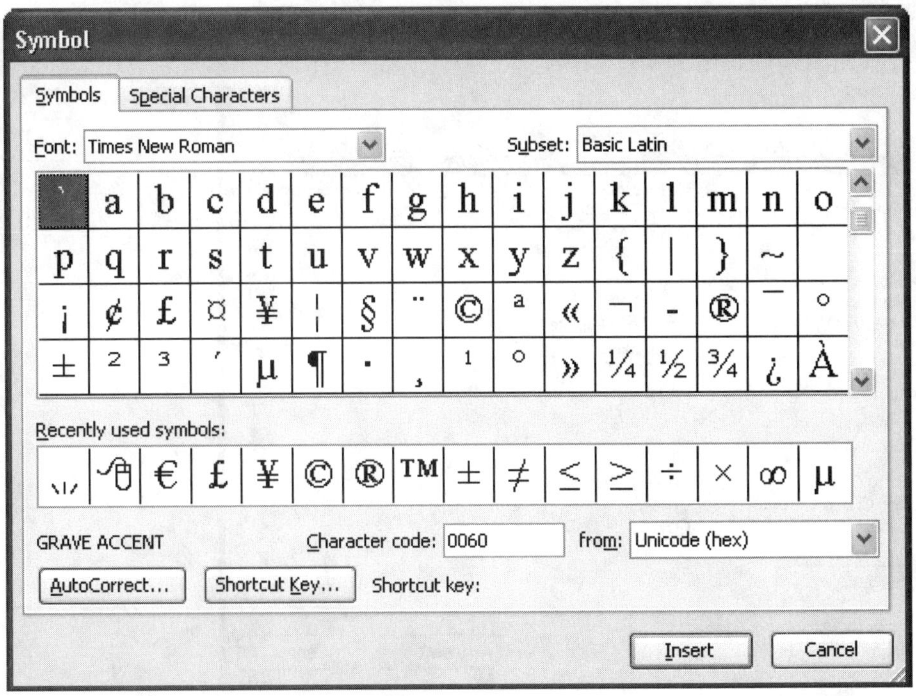

Figure 7-1: *The Symbol dialog box.*

Symbols as Pictures

Some fonts, such as Wingdings, are collections of symbols that are pictures. (See Figure 7-2.) When you insert the symbol in the document, because it is a text character, you can easily change its size or color to use the character as a picture in your document.

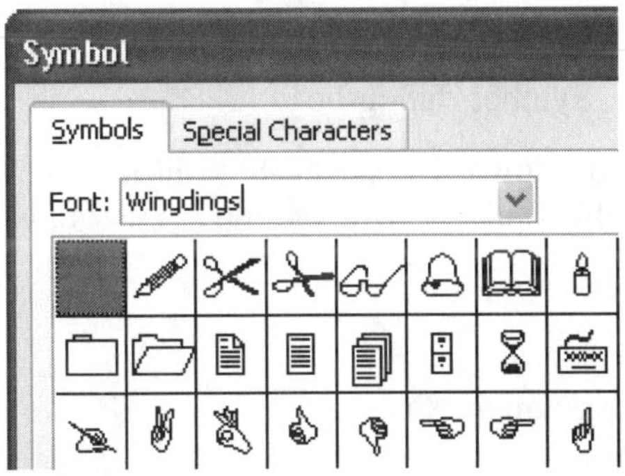

Figure 7-2: *Symbols as pictures using the Windings font.*

Special Characters

Special characters are uncommon punctuation, spacing, and typographical characters that are not readily available on the standard keyboard. A list of these can be found on the Special Characters tab in the Symbol dialog box. (See Figure 7-3.)

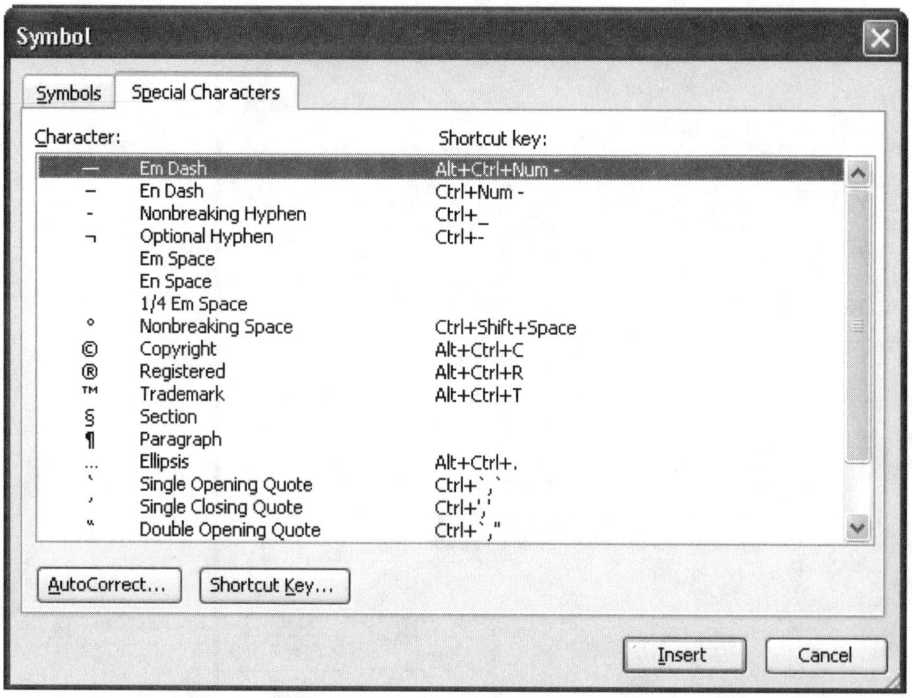

Figure 7-3: *The Special Characters tab in the Symbol dialog box.*

How to Insert Symbols and Special Characters

Procedure Reference: Insert a Symbol

To insert a symbol:

1. Place the insertion point where you want to insert the symbol.
2. Choose Insert→Symbol to display the Symbol dialog box.
3. On the Symbols tab, from the Font drop-down list, select the font that includes the symbol you want to use. The Symbols palette displays the symbols available for that font.
4. Select the desired symbol.
5. Click Insert to add the symbol to the document.

   You can also double-click a symbol to insert it.

6. Click Close.

Procedure Reference: Insert a Special Character

To insert a special character:

1. Place the insertion point where you want to insert the special character.
2. Choose Insert→Symbol to display the Symbol dialog box.
3. On the Special Characters tab, select the desired character.
4. Click Insert to insert the special character in the document.

You can also double-click a special character to insert it.

5. Click Close.

ACTIVITY 7-1

Inserting Symbols and Special Characters

Data Files:

- Rates of Interest.doc

Setup:

No documents are open.

Scenario:

You've finished drafting a company newsletter called "Rates of Interest." In the Legal Information text, the company style guide requires a registered trademark character immediately following the "Rates of Interest" publication name, and a copyright character between the word "copyright" and the year that the document was published. Furthermore, the style guide requires that the word "Phone" be replaced by a Wingdings telephone symbol in the "Contact Information" text.

What You Do	How You Do It
1. In the Legal Information paragraph of the Rates of Interest document, after the publication title, "Rates of Interest," **insert a registered trademark special character.** ·*Rates·of·Interest*®is·a·	a. **Open Rates of Interest.** b. Near the end of the Legal Information paragraph, **place the insertion point after the italicized word, "Interest."** ·*Rates·of·Interest*is·a· c. **Choose Insert→Symbol** to display the Symbol dialog box. d. **Select the Special Characters tab.**

e. In the Character list box, **select Registered.**

® Registered Alt+Ctrl+R

f. **Click Insert** to place the registered trademark symbol in the text.

g. **Click Close.**

---

2. In the same paragraph, **insert a copyright special character between the word "Copyright" and the year "2003."**

·copyright·©·2003.

a. **Place the insertion point just before the year "2003."**

·copyright·2003.·

b. **Choose Insert→Symbol and select the Special Characters tab.**

c. In the Character list box, **select Copyright and click Insert.**

d. **Click Close, and then press the Spacebar** to separate the copyright character from the year.

---

3. **Replace the word "Phone" with a Wingdings telephone symbol.**

a. Under "Contact Information," **select "Phone."**

Phone→(617)·555-8100¶

b. **Display the Symbols tab.** (Choose Insert→Symbol.)

c. From the Font drop-down list, **select Wingdings.**

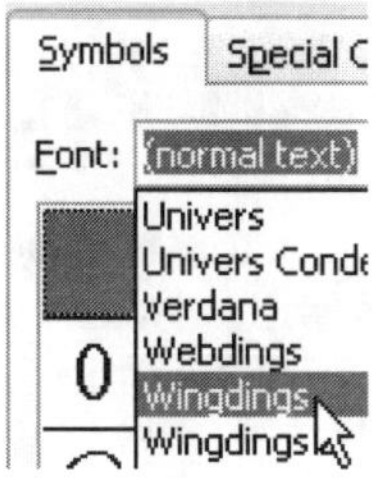

d. In the first row of the symbols area, **select the Telephone icon in the first row.**

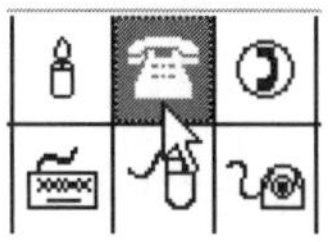

e. **Click Insert.**

The symbol is added to the Recently Used Symbols list and inserted into the text.

f. **Click Close.**

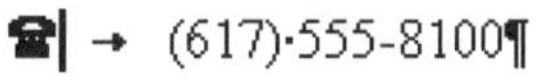

Remember, symbols are just text characters. So you can increase the font size of any symbol to make it more legible.

4. **Save the document as *My Rates of Interest***

TOPIC B

Insert a Clip Art Picture

You are not limited to inserting just text symbols and special characters to add visual interest to your documents. Word comes with a wide variety of colorful graphics you can use. In this topic, you will insert one of these pictures into a document.

You've added as much text formatting as you can without it becoming a distraction, yet the document still needs something. You want to add another visual element—a picture—but you haven't drawn anything since the third grade. And even if you were an artist, you don't have time to draw anything now. You just want a simple image that you can place in the document to support the text's message. Word provides an extensive catalog of professionally created pictures that you can add to your documents to make them more memorable.

Clip Art Task Pane

Use the Clip Art task pane to search for media files, or clips, stored on your computer and the Web. You search for clip art, photographs, movies, and sound files. Entering a word or phrase that describes the clip you want to find and clicking the Go button returns found clips in the Results area. (See Figure 7-4.)

Figure 7-4: *The Clip Art task pane.*

Resize Clips

When you select a clip in a document, small black squares called *selection handles* appear around the edges of the clip. (See Figure 7-5.) Dragging the clip's top and side selection handles stretches it. Dragging the clip's corner selection handles proportionally resizes the clip.

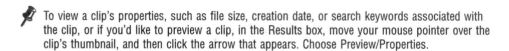

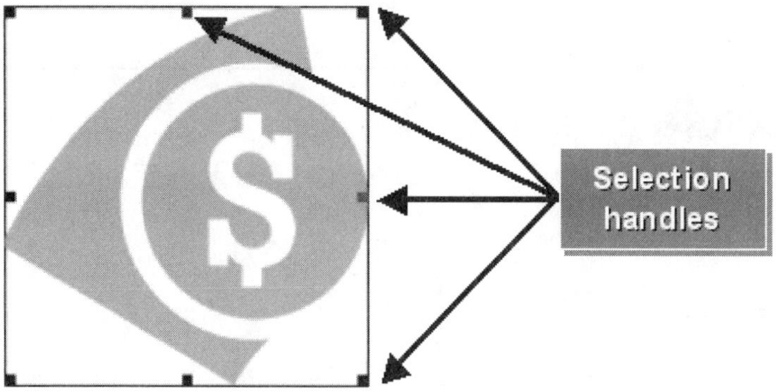

Figure 7-5: *Use selection handles to resize clips to fit better on a page.*

How to Insert a Clip Art Picture

Procedure Reference: Insert a Clip Art Picture

To insert a clip art picture:

1. Place the insertion point where you want to insert the clip art picture.
2. Choose Insert→Picture→Clip Art to display the Clip Art task pane.
3. In the Clip Art task pane's Search For text box, type a word or phrase that describes the clip art you want to locate.
4. If necessary, focus the search.
   - To reduce the number of locations to search, select a location from the Search In drop-down list.
   - Or, to specify the type of clips to find, use the Results Should Be drop-down list.
5. Click Go to begin the search.
6. In the Results area, click the desired clip to insert it.

   To view a clip's properties, such as file size, creation date, or search keywords associated with the clip, or if you'd like to preview a clip, in the Results box, move your mouse pointer over the clip's thumbnail, and then click the arrow that appears. Choose Preview/Properties.

7. Use the inserted picture's selection handles to resize the picture as needed.

Procedure Reference: Proportionally Resize a Picture

To maintain a picture's proportions as you resize it:

1. Select the picture.
2. Place the mouse pointer over one of the picture's corner selection handles.
3. Click and drag the corner selection handle until the picture is the desired size.
4. Release the mouse button to set the picture at its new size.

ACTIVITY 7-2

Inserting a Clip Art Picture

Setup:

My Rates of Interest is open.

Scenario:

Since the My Rates of Interest document is going to be a monetary guide frequently used by your co-workers and their clients, you want the document to be instantly identifiable, so they can refer to it quickly. You decide that adding a simple, money-oriented picture to the top of the document would help accomplish that, while at the same time reinforcing the text's financial message.

What You Do	How You Do It
1. With the insertion point at the beginning of the document, **display the Clip Art task pane.**	a. **Place the insertion point at the beginning of the document.**
	b. **Choose Insert→Picture→Clip Art** to display the Clip Art task pane.

2. **Search for clip art pictures related to "money."**

a. In the Search For text box, **type *Money***

b. From the Results Should Be drop-down list, **uncheck Photographs, Movies, and Sounds** to find only clip art pictures.

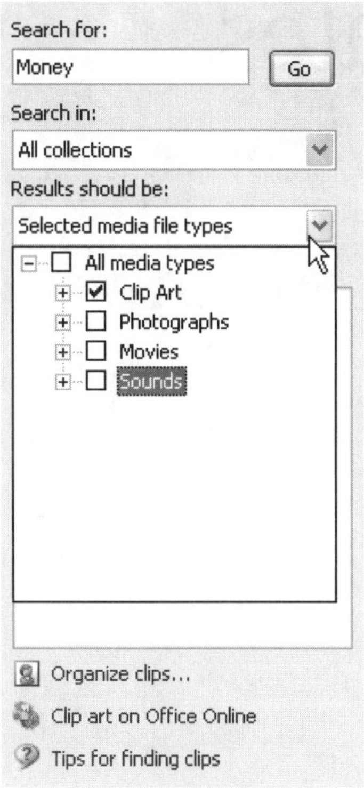

c. To close the drop-down list, **click the Results Should Be drop-down list arrow again.**

d. To the right of the Search For text box, **click Go** to locate and display clip art pictures related to money in the Results area.

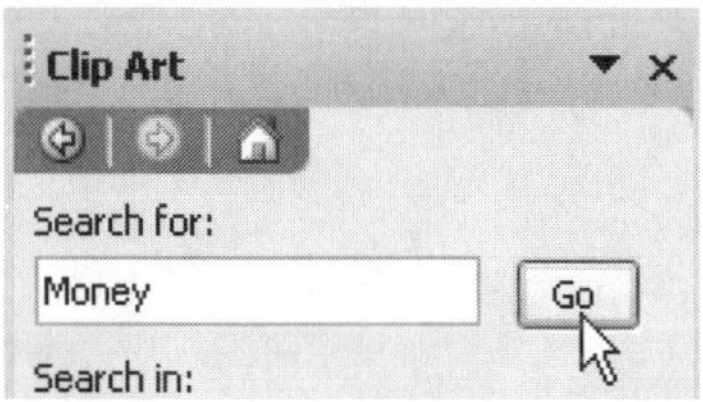

3. **Insert the dollar-sign clip art picture and proportionally size it so that it's about the same size as the "Rates of Interest" title.**

a. In the Results area of the Clip Art task pane, **click the dollar-sign picture** to insert it into the text.

It's a square-shaped piece of clip art, about 2 inches in size.

b. **Select the picture.**

c. **Notice that eight selection handles are displayed around the picture's edges.**

Whenever you select a picture, the Picture toolbar displays automatically.

d. **Place the mouse pointer over the picture's lower-right corner until the mouse pointer turns into a double-headed arrow.**

e. **Click and drag the corner selection handle until the picture is about a one-half inch square.**

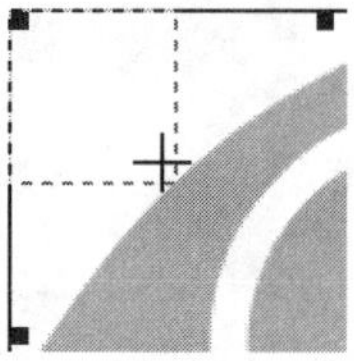

Use the horizontal and vertical rulers to help you judge the picture's size.

f. **Release the mouse button and deselect the clip art.**

4. **Close the Clip Art task pane.**

TOPIC C

Add a Watermark

Graphic elements may add visual interest to a document, but they can also be used to help identify a document's ownership or status. In this topic, you will add a watermark to identify a document's status.

Your manager calls you into her office. She just heard from a client who is irate because a product that you are writing about has been leaked to the press. "How could that have happened?", she demands to know. After a moment's thought, you realize that because your usual printer was busy, you used the Marketing department's printer—the same printer they use to print final press releases! Someone from that department must have accidentally released the document, thinking it was final. Even though it was an honest mistake, the damage has been done. This entire situation could have been avoided if the document was clearly marked confidential.

Watermarks

A *watermark* is a graphical element that, when printed, appears behind a document's text. Watermarks, whether a picture or text, can be used as a subtle way to identify a document's status, urgency, or ownership. (See Figure 7-6.)

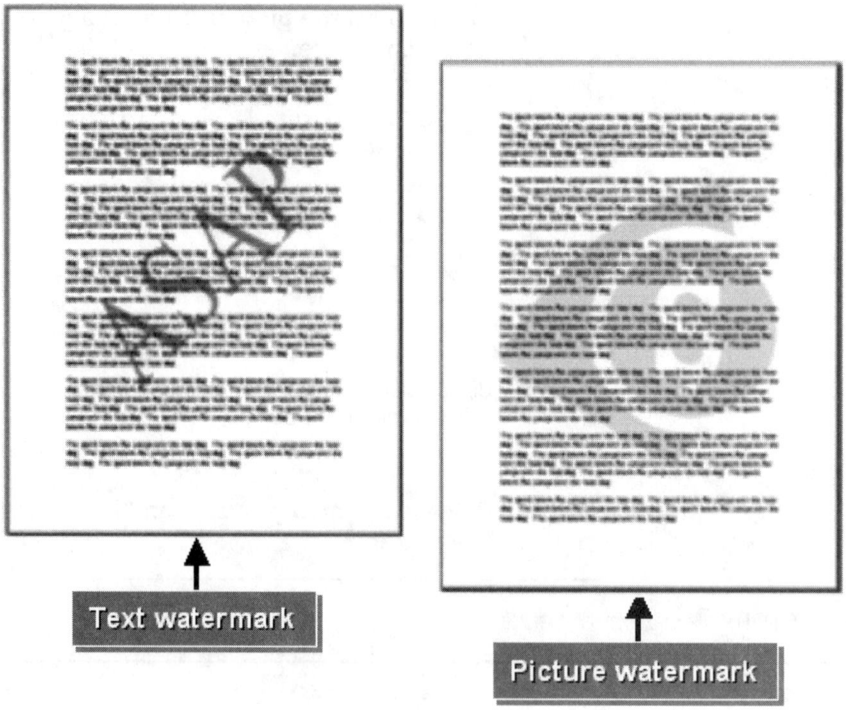

Figure 7-6: *Examples of watermarks.*

In Word, you can see watermarks only in Print Layout view.

How to Add a Watermark to a Document

Procedure Reference: Add a Text Watermark

To add a text watermark:

1. Choose Format→Background→Printed Watermark to display the Printed Watermark dialog box.
2. Select Text Watermark.
3. In the Text drop-down list box, type the text you want to appear as a watermark or select from the existing text items, such as CONFIDENTIAL.
4. Select other desired settings such as Font, Size, Color, and Layout options.
5. Click OK to insert the text watermark.

Text Watermark Options

You can adjust a variety of common text options—Font, Size, and Color. You can also determine whether or not the text will be semitransparent. Selected by default, the Semitransparent option affects the text watermark opacity. The Semitransparent option lightens the watermark so that the document text remains legible. You can also determine whether or not the text watermark will be displayed horizontally from left to right or diagonally (from the lower-left corner of the page to the upper-right corner of the page.) Again, it's recommended that Diagonal, the default, be left selected for the best results.

Procedure Reference: Add a Picture Watermark

To add a picture watermark:

1. Choose Format→Background→Printed Watermark to display the Printed Watermark dialog box.
2. Select Picture Watermark.
3. Click Select Picture and navigate to where the picture is located.
4. Select the picture and click Insert.
5. Select any other desired options, such as Scale and Washout.
6. Click OK to insert the picture watermark.

Picture Watermark Options

You can adjust a couple picture watermark options. Scale allows you to resize the picture proportionally. You can also use Washout to make the picture appear semitransparent, so the document's text isn't obscured on the screen or when printed.

Procedure Reference: Remove a Watermark

To remove a watermark from a document:

1. Choose Format→Background→Printed Watermark.
2. Select No Watermark.
3. Click OK.

ACTIVITY 7-3

Adding a Text Watermark

Setup:

My Rates of Interest is open.

Scenario:

The My Rates of Interest document is ready to be reviewed. However, the last time you sent something for review, it was printed without your approval, and several thousand copies had to be thrown away. To ensure that doesn't happen again, you could mark the document as an INTERNAL DRAFT, so that there is no question about the document's current status.

What You Do	How You Do It
1. **Apply an "INTERNAL DRAFT" text watermark** to the document.	a. **Choose Format→Background→Printed Watermark** to display the Printed Watermark dialog box.
	b. **Select Text Watermark.**
	c. **Display the Text drop-down list.**
	d. There isn't an INTERNAL DRAFT option so you need to type it. In the Text drop-down list box, **type *INTERNAL DRAFT*** 
	e. **Click OK** to add the text watermark to the document's background.
2. **How might you want to change the text watermark?**	
3. **How might you use watermarks in your documents?**	
4. If you are not going to perform the following practice activity, **save and close My Rates of Interest.**	

PRACTICE ACTIVITY 7-4

Applying a Confidential Text Watermark

Setup:

My Rates of Interest is open.

Scenario:

The My Rates of Interest document has been reviewed and approved. Mark it with a CONFIDENTIAL text watermark.

1. In My Rates of Interest, **change the text watermark from INTERNAL DRAFT to CONFIDENTIAL.**
2. **Save and close My Rates of Interest.**

Lesson 7 Follow-up

In this lesson, you added graphic elements to enhance a document. You inserted symbols and special characters to add visual interest as well as typographical accuracy. You inserted and manipulated a piece of clip art to support the text's message. Lastly, you applied a watermark to the document to brand the document as a way to identify its status.

1. **In your documents, how might you use symbols and special characters?**

2. **What is your opinion of clip art and do you intend to use it in your documents?**

Notes

LESSON 8

Controlling Page Appearance

Lesson Time
40 minutes

Lesson Objectives:

In this lesson, you will control a document's page setup and its overall appearance.

You will:

- Change the page orientation.
- Change margins.
- Apply a page border.
- Add a header and footer.
- Insert a page break.

Introduction

You have seen how to format individual elements—characters, paragraphs, and tables—in some common business documents. In this lesson, you will apply formatting that will affect an entire page.

When you create a document in Word, the content may not always fit on the page the way you want. By changing a variety of page options, you can get the content to fit, as well as enhance the document's appearance and readability.

TOPIC A

Set Page Orientation

Some documents, such as letters, are setup to use a "tall" page. Other documents, such as diplomas or awards, use a "wide" page. In this topic, you will change a document's page orientation.

You have a frame that hangs horizontally and you need to create a certificate to fit it. So you enter and format the text in a new document, print it, then use scissors to cut the text into strips. You then glue the text snippets on to a new sheet of paper that you've turned sideways. You then take your creation to the copier and make a copy of it so that the pasted blocks of text aren't so obvious. Sure you can do it that way, but you can save yourself a lot of time, hassle, and sticky fingers by just changing the page's orientation in Word—not to mention that the certificate will look much better.

Page Orientation

In Word, you can use the Page Setup dialog box to position a page either vertically or horizontally. (See Figure 8-1.) When a page is positioned vertically so that it is taller than it is wide, the page is said to have *portrait* orientation. When a page is positioned horizontally so that it is wider than it is tall, the page is said to have *landscape* orientation.

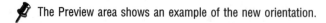

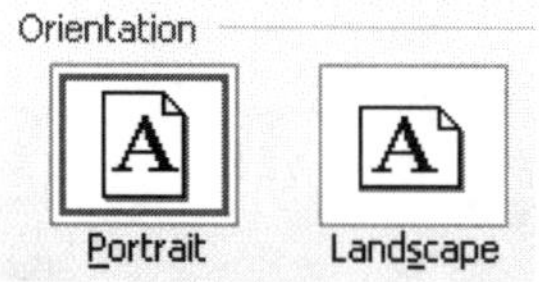

Figure 8-1: *Page orientation options.*

How to Set a Document's Page Orientation

Procedure Reference: Set a Document's Page Orientation

To set a document's page orientation:

1. Choose File→Page Setup.
2. On the Margins tab, under Orientation, select the desired page orientation (Portrait or Landscape).

The Preview area shows an example of the new orientation.

3. Click OK to set the page orientation.

Procedure Reference: Rename a Folder

To rename a folder in the Save As dialog box:

You can also rename folders in the Open dialog box.

1. Choose File→Save As.
2. Select the folder you want to rename.
3. Choose Tools→Rename.

   You can also right-click a folder and choose Rename or, with a folder selected, you can press F2 to rename it.

4. Type the new name.
5. Press Enter.

ACTIVITY 8-1

Changing a Document's Page Orientation

Data Files:

- Certificate Memo.doc

Setup:

No documents are open.

Scenario:

Your manager has put you in charge of creating a new sales certificate. (See the Certificate Memo for more details.) To begin the assignment, you decide to put the certificate text in a new landscape document. Then, as you save the document, you decide to rename the Awards folder as Certificates.

What You Do	How You Do It
1. From the Certificate Memo, **copy the certificate content and paste it into a new document.**	a. **Open Certificate Memo.** b. **Copy the paragraphs from "REGIONAL SALES" through "Principal Agent, Owner."** c. **Close Certificate Memo.** d. On the Standard toolbar, **click the New Blank Document button** . e. **Paste the copied text into the new document.**
2. **Set the new blank document's orientation to landscape and zoom out to display the whole page.**	a. **Choose File→Page Setup** to display the Page Setup dialog box. b. On the Margins tab, under Orientation, **select Landscape.** 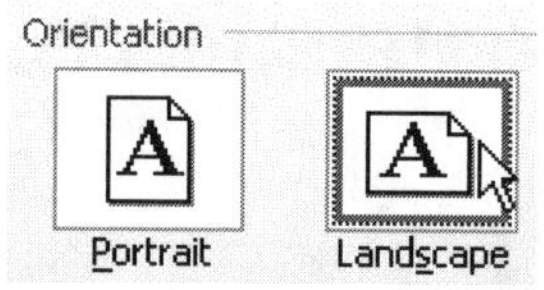 c. **Click OK** to set the new page orientation. d. On the Standard toolbar, from the Zoom drop-down list, **select Whole Page.** 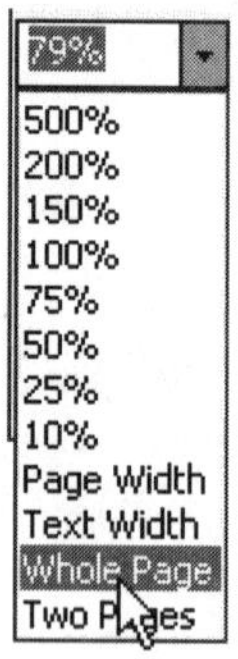

3. **Save the document to the newly renamed Certificates folder as *My Sales Certificate*.**

a. **Choose File→Save As.**

b. **Select the Awards folder.**

c. **Choose Tools→Rename.**

d. **Type *Certificates***

e. **Press Enter.**

f. **Double-click the Certificates folder** to **open it.**

g. In the File Name text box, **type *My Sales Certificate***

h. **Click Save.**

TOPIC B

Change Page Margins

Another way to control how much text appears on a page is to add or remove white space from around the edges of a document. In this topic, you will adjust the document's margins.

You've loaded some of the company's stationery into the printer and you're ready to print your letter. When printed, however, you notice that the text has printed over the stationery text, making both the stationery and the letter text illegible. By making the top margin in the document larger, the text will begin printing lower on the page, below the stationery text. Setting margins enables you to specify how much white space should display for the top, bottom, left, and right areas on each printed page.

How to Change Page Margins

Procedure Reference: Change Page Margins in the Page Setup Dialog Box

To change a page's margins using the Page Setup dialog box:

1. Choose File→Page Setup.

   In Print Layout view, you can double-click the shaded margin area of a ruler to display the Page Setup dialog box.

2. Select the Margins tab.

3. Under Margins, enter the desired measurements for the Top, Bottom, Left, and Right margins.
4. Click OK.

Change Page Margins Using the Rulers

Rather than use the Page Setup dialog box, you can change a page's margins by dragging the appropriate margin markers on the vertical and horizontal rulers. This is a useful method, especially when previewing a document, for making quick, if imprecise, changes to the top and bottom margins. However, adjusting the left and right margin markers is slightly more involved. They are obscured by the left and right indent markers, making it necessary to move the indent markers prior to dragging the left and right margin markers.

To specify exact margin measurements in the rulers, hold down Alt as you drag the margin boundary/marker.

Procedure Reference: Center Text Between the Top and Bottom Margins

To center text on a page between the top and bottom margins:

1. Choose File→Page Setup.
2. Select the Layout tab.
3. Under Page, from the Vertical Alignment drop-down list, select the Center.
4. Click OK.

Vertical Alignment Options

You have four vertical alignment options to choose from: Top, Center, Justified, and Bottom. As you might expect, the Top option positions the text along the top of the page. (Top is the default vertical alignment setting.) Bottom aligns text along the bottom of the page. The Center option positions the page's text in the center of the page, providing equal amounts of white space above and below the text. The Justified option adds equal amounts of white space between each paragraph, so the text appears to fill the page.

Vertical alignment options work the same way for either portrait or landscape page orientations.

ACTIVITY 8-2

Changing the Certificate's Margins

Setup:

Certificate Memo is closed. My Sales Certificate is open.

Scenario:

The top and bottom margins are slightly larger than the side margins and the certificate text is too close to the top of the page. So that there's an equal amount of white space surrounding the text, you decide to change the top and bottom margins to match the left and right margins while vertically centering the text on the page.

What You Do	How You Do It
1. **Change the top and bottom margins to 1 inch.**	a. **Choose File→Page Setup** to display the Page Setup dialog box.
	b. On the Margins tab, in the Top text box, **type *1***
	c. **Press Tab** to move to the Bottom text box.
	d. **Type *1*** 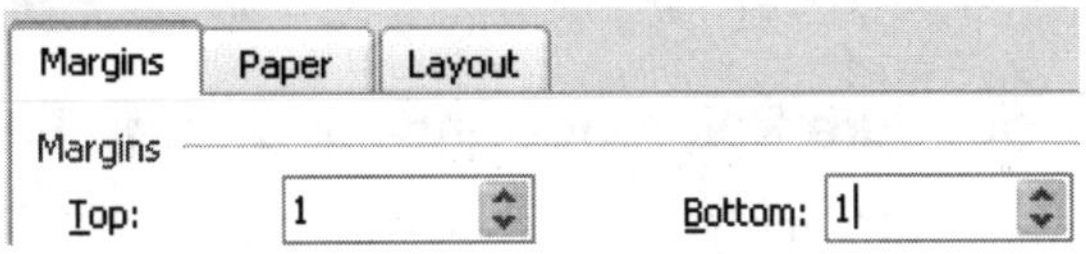
	e. **Click OK** to apply the new margin settings. The change is subtle as the text moves up a quarter of an inch.
2. **Center the certificate text vertically on the page.**	a. **Display the Page Setup dialog box.**
	b. **Select the Layout tab.**

c. From the Vertical Alignment drop-down list, **select Center.**

d. **Click OK.**

TOPIC C

Apply a Page Border

Another way to add visual interest to a document is to add a border around the outside of the page. In this topic, you will do that.

You've created a flyer announcing the company's holiday party. However, when you print the document and put it on the bulletin board in the break room, it doesn't stand out like you want. All the flyers on the board seem to blend together. How can you add visual interest to your document, while helping people stay focused as they read it? Add a page border.

How to Apply a Page Border

Procedure Reference: Apply a Page Border

To apply a border to a page:

1. In the Borders And Shading dialog box (Format→Borders And Shading), display the Page Border tab.

   You can also display the Page Border tab by choosing File→Page Setup, selecting the Layout tab, and clicking Borders.

2. Select a border type, either a line or art border.
3. Set border options.
   - For a line page border, select a Setting (None, Box, Shadow, 3-D, or Custom), a line style, color, and width.
   - Or, for an art page border, select an art border from the Art drop-down list, and set color and width options.

     If the art border is black and white, you can modify its color.

4. If necessary, in the Preview area, click the border buttons to add or remove them, creating a Custom Setting.
5. Click OK to apply the border.

Art Options

Word provides dozens of seasonal and professional Art page borders that can serve as printed frames for certificates, awards, or diplomas. When you select an Art page border, it's applied as a Box or Custom style. You can also adjust the size of the art in the border by modifying its width.

ACTIVITY 8-3

Applying an Art Page Border

Setup:

My Sales Certificate is open.

Scenario:

You want to get a bit more creative and add visual interest to the sales certificate.

What You Do	How You Do It
1. In the Borders And Shading dialog box, **display the Page Border tab.**	a. **Choose Format→Borders And Shading.** b. **Select the Page Border tab.**
2. **Apply an art page border made up of green houses to the top and bottom of the page.**	a. From the Art drop-down list, about half way down, **select the Houses border.**

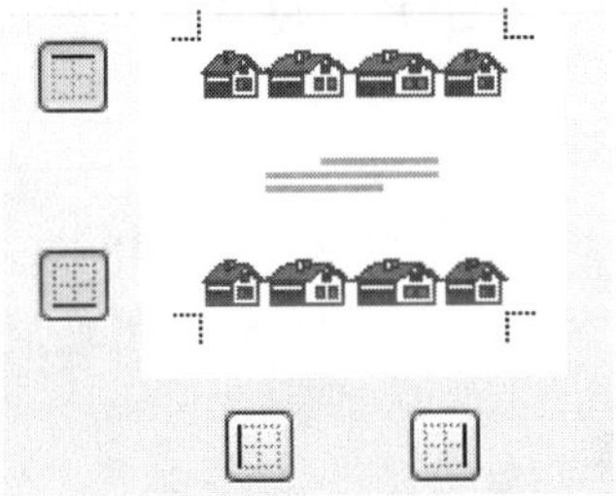

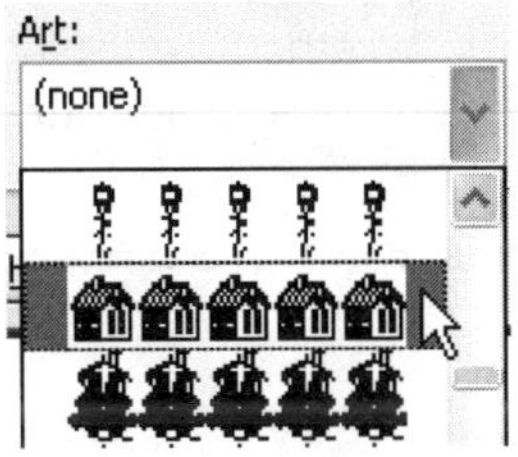

The Box setting and Width are automatically selected.

b. From the Color drop-down list, **change the color to Green.**

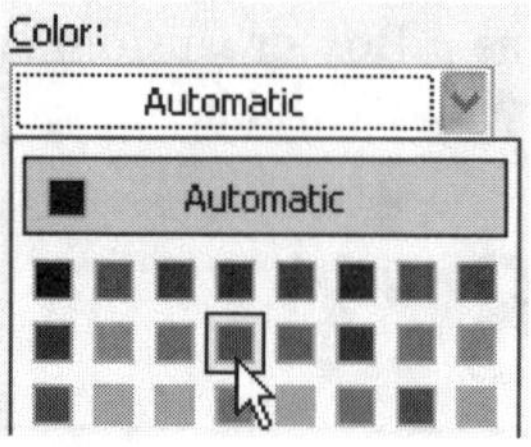

c. In the Preview area, **click the Left Border button** to turn it off.

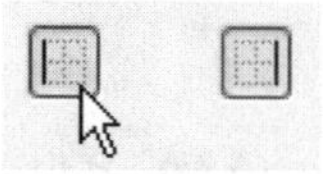

The Preview is updated to show the change and the Setting has changed from Box to Custom.

d. **Click the Right Border button** to turn it off.

e. **Click OK** to apply the art border to the top and bottom of the certificate.

3. If you are not going to complete the following practice activity, **save and close My Sales Certificate.**

PRACTICE ACTIVITY 8-4

Changing the Art Border

Scenario:

Your manager wants the certificate to reflect the fact that the person is a star performer. The border you've chosen doesn't meet this requirement.

1. **Change the page's art border to 30 pt stars.**
2. **Save and close My Sales Certificate.**

TOPIC D

Add Headers and Footers

Margins can be used to add white space to a document. However, the top and bottom margins can also be used to contain useful information that you want repeated on every page. In this topic, you will add such content in a document's header and footer.

You just got back from a trade show and have a stack of papers to review. One article in particular is very interesting, but nowhere in the document is there any indication of who wrote it or how many pages it is. You figure then that it must be a section that fell out of some other document you got. After an hour of comparing the article's formatting to other documents in the pile, you deduce that it belongs in Acme Trust's research review. They wasted your time unnecessarily, and, weeks from now, you may not remember the article, but you will probably remember that Acme aggravated you. The folks at Acme could have easily improved the document by adding page numbers and other useful information to the header and footer area.

Headers and Footers

A *header* is the blank area in a page's top margin and a *footer* is the blank area in a page's bottom margin. Headers and footers can contain textual or graphical information to provide context for the reader. Common header and footer information includes titles, dates, and page numbers.

Header And Footer Toolbar

Use the Header And Footer Toolbar to add information to the header and footer areas quickly, as well as to navigate between them. (See Figure 8-2.)

Figure 8-2: *The Header And Footer toolbar.*

Fields

A *field* is a set of instructions used to dynamically display specific pieces of information, such as the current date, time, or page number. When Word encounters a field, it is interpreted and the field's results are automatically displayed within the field.

When the insertion point is within a field, the field's background turns gray to help identify it as a field.

To show a field's code, place the insertion point in the field result and press Shift+F9.

Fields in Headers and Footers

A common location for fields is in a document's header and footer areas. You can use the Header and Footer toolbar to insert fields quickly to show the current page number, total number of pages in the document, date, and time.

How to Add Headers and Footers

Procedure Reference: Add Headers and Footers

To add headers and footers to a document:

1. Choose View→Header And Footer to display the header area and the Header And Footer toolbar.

   Word switches the view to Print Layout view, if necessary, to display headers and footers.

2. Add and format information in the header area.
3. On the Header And Footer toolbar, click the Switch Between Header And Footer button  to move the insertion point to the footer.
4. Add and format information in the footer area.
5. On the Header And Footer toolbar, click Close to close the header and footer area and review the header and footer in Print Layout view.

Procedure Reference: Modify Headers and Footers

To change the contents of a header or footer:

1. In Print Layout view, double-click the header or footer area you want to modify.

   You can also choose View→Header And Footer.

2. Make the desired changes.
3. On the Header And Footer toolbar, click Close.

Procedure Reference: Change Page Number Formats

To change page number formats:

1. Display the header or footer containing the page number.

2. On the Header And Footer toolbar, click the Format Page Number button  to display the Page Number Format dialog box.
3. From the Number Format drop-down list, select the desired format.
4. Click OK to set the new format.

Page Number Format Options

Using the Header And Footer toolbar, you can change the page number formats from the default "1, 2, 3" format to any of the following Arabic or Roman numeral formats:

- -1-, -2-, -3-,...
- a, b, c,...
- A, B, C,...
- i, ii, iii,...
- I, II, III,...

ACTIVITY 8-5

Adding a Header and a Footer

Data Files:

- Annual Overview.doc

Setup:

No documents are open.

Scenario:

Your manager is giving a presentation at the Relo Expo conference and would like to leave the company's annual overview behind as a handout so potential clients can peruse last year's successes. Your job is to make the handout more identifiable as a Burke Properties document and to make it easier for the people to read.

What You Do	How You Do It
1. In the header area of the Annual Overview document, **type and center *Burke Properties Annual Overview*.**	a. From the My Documents folder, **open Annual Overview.**
	b. **Choose View→Header And Footer.**
	Word grays out the document text and places the insertion point in the header area.
	c. **Press Tab once** to move the insertion point to the center tab.
	You can also click the Center button on the Formatting toolbar.
	d. **Type *Burke Properties Annual Overview***
	Take a moment to review the Insert AutoText drop-down list options on the Header And Footer toolbar.

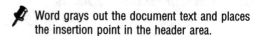

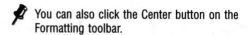

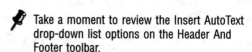

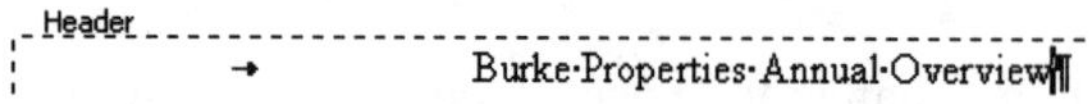

2. **Add a footer that includes the conference name, as well as the current date and time on the left and the page number on the right.**

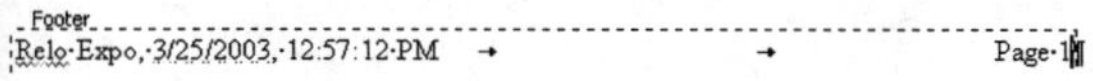

a. To move the insertion point to the footer area, **click the Switch Between Header And Footer button** .

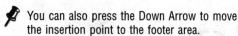

You can also press the Down Arrow to move the insertion point to the footer area.

b. **Type *Relo Expo***

c. **Type a comma (,) and press the Spacebar.**

d. On the Header And Footer toolbar, **click the Insert Date button** .

e. **Type a comma (,) and press the Spacebar.**

f. **Click the Insert Time button** to add the current time field to the footer area.

g. **Press Tab twice** to move the insertion point to the right-aligned tab.

h. **Type *Page* and press the Spacebar.**

i. **Click the Insert Page Number button** to insert the automatic page numbering field.

---

3. **Preview the new header and footer content.**

a. On the Header And Footer toolbar, **click Close.**

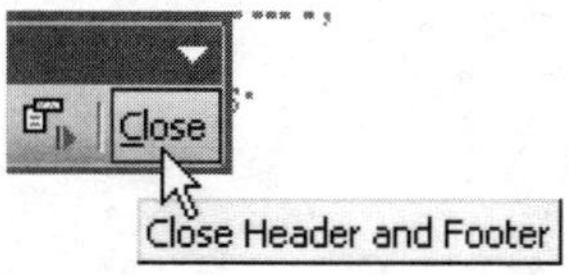

Headers and footers are visible only in Print Layout view or Print Preview.

b. **Display the document in Print Preview** to see the header and footer text.

c. **Close Print Preview** to return to Print Layout view.

---

4. **Save the document in My Documents as *My Annual Overview***

ACTIVITY 8-6

Modifying Headers and Footers

Setup:

My Annual Overview is open.

Scenario:

Rather than use the annual overview as a handout at the conference, it will be included in the front matter of the Burke Properties Annual Report instead. You will need to make sure that the overview blends with the annual report. The header text reflects the title and the footer has a page number field.

What You Do	How You Do It
1. In the header area of the My Annual Overview document, **change the text to read *Burke Properties Annual Report*.**	a. At the top of the document, **double-click the header area** to edit the text in the header area. b. **Select the word "Overview" and type *Report***
2. **Edit the footer so it displays only a centered page number field formatted as a lower-case Roman numeral.** 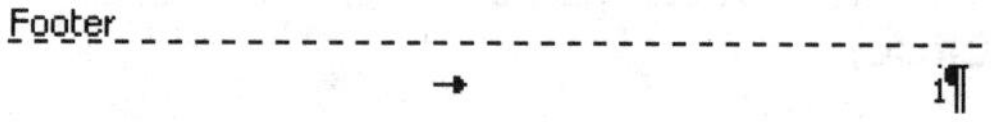	a. **Switch to the footer.** b. **Delete all the text in the footer area.** c. **Press Tab and click Insert Page Number** to add the page number field to the footer. d. **Click the Format Page Number button** to display the Page Number Format dialog box.

e. From the Number Format drop-down list, **select the i, ii, iii option.**

f. **Click OK** to format the page number.

g. **Close the header and footer areas.**

TOPIC E

Insert a Page Break

Sometimes you may want to force some text to move to its own page so that it will be printed on a separate page. You can control where text breaks across pages in your documents. In this topic, you will insert a page break.

The report you're working on has four different topics. On paper, the titles of the shorter topics printed at the bottom of one page, with the headings' related paragraphs on the next. It took some doing, but you were able to add just the right number of blank lines before the heading to push it to the next page. You then had to repeat that task for the remaining topics to ensure that they didn't have the same "split" problem. It would be better if you could control exactly where one page ends and where another begins to prevent awkward content divisions and to keep related content on the same page. Manual page breaks can do just that.

Automatic Versus Manual Page Breaks

When there's too much text to fit on a single page, Word inserts automatic, or soft, page breaks to accommodate the additional text. There may be times, however, when you want to control where a page ends. In those cases, you can insert a manual, or hard, page break. Manual page breaks appear as a non-printing, dotted line with the words "Page Break" in the middle of the line. (See Figure 8-3.)

Automatic page breaks are primarily determined by margin settings in the Page Setup dialog box.

The appearance of automatic page breaks depends on the view in which the document is displayed.

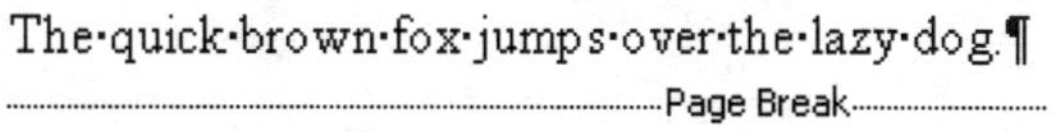

Figure 8-3: *A manual page break.*

How to Insert a Manual Page Break

Procedure Reference: Insert a Page Break Manually

To insert a manual page break:

Press Ctrl+Enter to quickly insert a manual page break at the insertion point.

1. Place the insertion point where you want the new page to begin.
2. Choose Insert→Break to display the Break dialog box.
3. Select Page Break, if necessary.
4. Click OK to insert the manual page break.

Procedure Reference: Hide White Space

In Print Layout view, the top and bottom margins of a page can sometimes get in the way when you're trying to view text at the bottom of one page and the text at the top of the next page at the same time. To hide white space between pages in Print Layout view:

Hiding white space also hides headers and footers.

1. Place the mouse pointer over the automatic page break between two pages.
2. Click the mouse button once to hide the white space between the two pages. (Click the mouse button again to show the white space.)

Procedure Reference: Delete a Manual Page Break

As you write or edit a document, you will likely change its length, perhaps making one or more manual page breaks unnecessary. To delete a manual page break:

1. If desired, switch to Normal view.

   It is often easier to work with manual page breaks in Normal view.

2. Place the insertion point on the same line as the manual page break that you want to delete.

   You can use the Special option in the Find And Replace dialog box to locate manual page breaks.

3. Press Delete.
4. If necessary, switch back to Print Layout view.

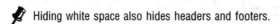

ACTIVITY 8-7

Using Manual Page Breaks

Setup:

My Annual Overview is open.

Scenario:

The Annual Report's editor says you can use three pages for the overview text. So your manager would like to reserve an entire page for both the Financial and the Future Objectives topics. To accomplish that, you need to hide the white space between pages to make it easier for you to use manual page breaks to push the individual topics on to their own pages.

What You Do	How You Do It
1. **How many pages are in the document currently?**_	
2. **Insert a manual page break before the "Financial" heading.**	a. Near the bottom of page i, **place the insertion point before the "F" in the "Financial" heading.**
	b. **Choose Insert→Break** to display the Break dialog box.
	c. Under Break Types, **verify that Page Break is selected.**

d. To insert a manual page break and push the Financial heading and its related text to the next page, **click OK.**

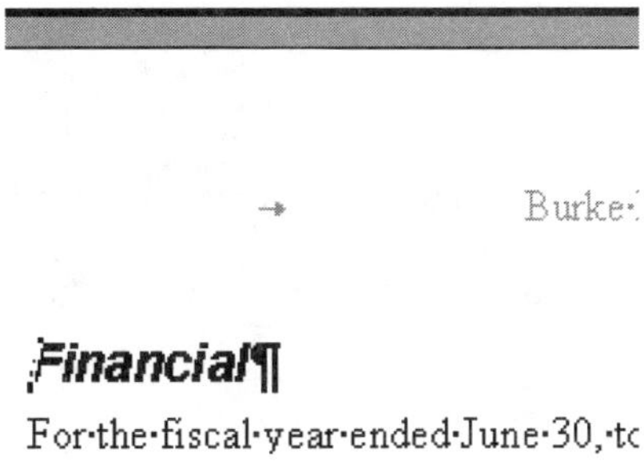

3. **Insert a manual page break before the "Future Objectives" heading.**

   a. On page ii, **place the insertion point to the left of the "F" in the "Future Objectives" heading.**

   b. To push the "Future Objectives" heading to page three, **press Ctrl+Enter.**

   c. **Notice that the status bar now shows that there are three pages in the document.**

   The header and footer are automatically added to the new page.

---

4. **Hide the white space between page 2 and page 3.**

   a. **Position the mouse pointer over the automatic page break between pages 2 and 3** to display the Hide White Space icon.

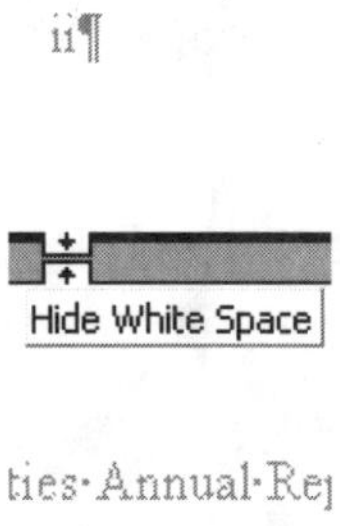

   b. **Click once** to hide the footer on page 2 and the header on page 3, as well as the extra white space.

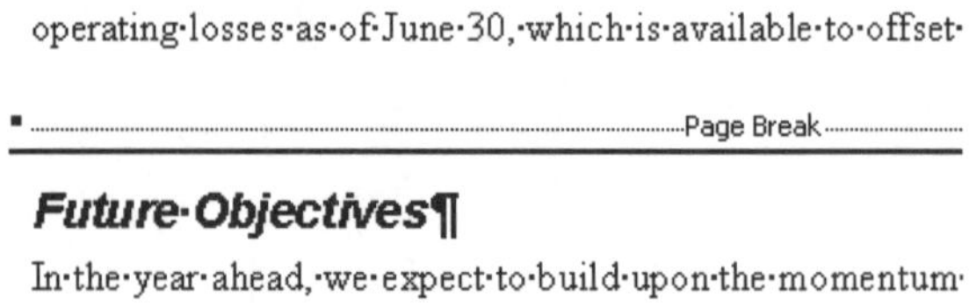

operating·losses·as·of·June·30,·which·is·available·to·offset·
Page Break
Future·Objectives¶
In·the·year·ahead,·we·expect·to·build·upon·the·momentum·

   The new page break cleanly separates the Financial and Future Objectives text.

---

5. **Redisplay the white space between page 2 and page 3.**

   a. **Position the mouse pointer over the automatic page break between pages 2 and 3** to display the Show White Space icon.

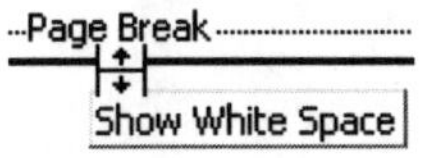

   b. **Click the mouse button once** to redisplay the footer, header, and white space.

ACTIVITY 8-8

Deleting a Manual Page Break

Scenario:

The Annual Report's editor called and they need the extra page. Therefore, you have to return the overview to two pages.

What You Do	How You Do It
1. In Normal view, **delete the manual page break at the bottom of page 2.**	a. To make it easier to work with the manual page break, **switch to Normal view.**

Choose View→Normal.

b. Above the Future Objectives heading, **place the insertion point on the same line as the manual page break.**

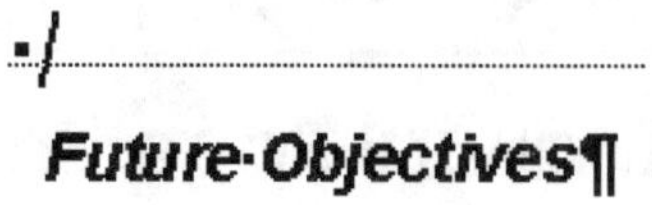

c. **Press Delete** to get rid of the manual page break and return the document to two pages.

d. **Switch back to Print Layout view.**

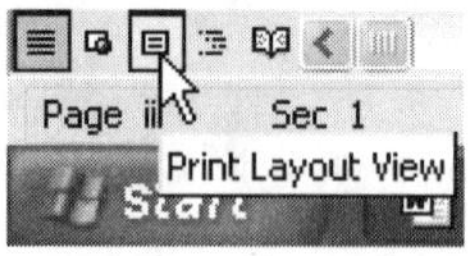

2. **How many pages is the document now?**_

3. **Save and close My Annual Overview.**

Lesson 8 Follow-up

In this lesson, you used a variety of page setup methods to arrange content on the page so that it's displayed the way you want it. You set the page orientation, changed margin settings, added headers and footers, applied page borders, and inserted page breaks. These skills will help you put the finishing touches on any document.

1. **Think about the types of documents you will be working with—perhaps a letter, report, handout, minutes, or itinerary. How might you take advantage of the various page layout options to enhance the printed document?**

2. **Considering how you work, do you anticipate modifying a document's page setup options when you first create a document or waiting until you are almost finished with a document? Why?**

FOLLOW-UP

Follow-up

In this course you created, edited, and enhanced standard documents using Microsoft® Word 2003.

1. **Which feature in Word will help the most as you create documents?**

2. **What automatic features in Word will you use most often?**

3. **How will you use Word's Help options?**

What's Next?

After completing this course, students may be interested in expanding their knowledge of Microsoft® Word 2003 by taking Element K's *Microsoft Word 2003: Level 2* and *Microsoft Word 2003: Level 3* courses.

APPENDIX A

Microsoft Office Specialist Program

Selected Element K courseware addresses Microsoft Office Specialist skills. The following tables indicate where Word 2003 skills are covered. For example, 1-3 indicates the lesson and activity number applicable to that skill.

Core Skill Sets and Skills Being Measured	Word 2003: Level 1	Word 2003: Level 2	Word 2003: Level 3
Insert and edit text, symbols and special characters			
Inserting text, symbols, hidden text and special characters	1-4, 2-3, 7-1, 1-Lab, 2-Lab, 5-Lab	8-2	5-3
Deleting, cutting, copying, pasting text and using the clipboard	2-6, 2-7, 2-8, 2-Lab		
Checking spelling and grammar	5-3, 4-Lab		
Checking language usage (e.g., Thesaurus)	5-1, 5-Lab		
Insert Frequently Used and Pre-defined Text			
Creating text for repeated use (e.g., AutoText)	2-5		
Inserting pre-defined text (e.g., AutoText and AutoCorrect)	1-4, 2-5		
Inserting date and time fields	8-5		
Navigate to Specific Content			
Finding and replacing text	2-10	2-Lab	
Moving to selected content (e.g., Select Browse Object, Go To)			2-8, 3-3
Insert, Position, and Size Graphics			
Inserting, positioning, and sizing graphics, text boxes, and shapes	7-2, 6-Lab	6-1, 6-2, 6-3, 7-3, 5-Lab, 6-Lab	
Create and Modify Diagrams and Charts			

Core Skill Sets and Skills Being Measured	Word 2003: Level 1	Word 2003: Level 2	Word 2003: Level 3
Creating and modifying charts and diagrams		2-7, 2-8, 6-4, 2-Lab	
Locate, Select, and Insert Supporting Information			
Locating supporting information in local reference materials or on the Internet using the Research too.	5-1		1-6
Using the Research tool to select and insert supporting text-based information	5-1		1-6
Insert and Modify Tables			
Inserting new tables	6-1, 6-Lab		
Converting text to tables	6-6, 6-Lab		
Applying pre-defined formats to tables (e.g., Autoformats)	6-5, 6-Lab		
Modifying table borders and shading	6-5	2-5	
Revising tables (insert and delete rows and columns, modify cell formats)		2-2, 2-Lab	
Create Bulleted Lists, Numbered Lists, and Outlines			
Customizing and applying bullets and numbering	4-6	1-4, 1-5	
Creating outlines		1-4	
Insert and Modify Hyperlinks			
Inserting and modifying hyperlinks to other documents and Web pages			6-2
Format Text			
Finding and modifying font typeface, style, color and size	3-7, 3-Lab	4-1, 4-Lab	
Applying styles to and clearing styles from text, tables, and lists	3-6, 4-5, 4-Lab	4-1, 4-3, 4-4, 4-Lab	
Applying highlights to text	3-4, 3-Lab		
Applying text effects		3-2, 3-Lab	
Modifying character spacing		3-1	
Format Paragraphs			
Applying borders and shading to paragraphs	4-4, 4-Lab		
Indenting, spacing, and aligning paragraphs	4-2, 4-3, 4-7, 4-Lab	2-Lab	
Setting, removing, and modifying tab stops	4-1, 4-Lab		
Apply and Format Columns			
Applying and formatting columns		7-2, 7-Lab	

Core Skill Sets and Skills Being Measured	Word 2003: Level 1	Word 2003: Level 2	Word 2003: Level 3
Insert and Modify Content in Headers and Footers			
Inserting and modifying content in document headers and footers	8-5, 8-Lab	8-2	
Inserting and formatting page numbers	8-5, 8-6		
Modify Document Layout and Page Setup			
Inserting and deleting breaks	2-3, 8-7, 8-8	7-1, 7-2, 7-Lab	
Modifying page margins and page orientation	8-1, 8-2, 8-Lab		
Circulate Documents for Review			
Sending documents for review via e-mail			2-4
Sending documents in an e-mail or as an e-mail attachment			1-7, 1-Lab
Compare and Merge Documents			
Comparing and merging documents			2-6, 2-7, 2-Lab
Insert, View, and Edit Comments			
Inserting, viewing, and editing comments			2-5, 2-8, 2-Lab
Track, Accept, and Reject Proposed Changes			
Locating successive changes in a document			2-8, 2-Lab
Tracking, accepting, and rejecting changes			2-5, 2-8, 2-Lab
Create New Documents Using Templates			
Creating new document types using templates		9-1, 9-3, 9-Lab	
Review and Modify Document Properties			
Reviewing and modifying the document summary			2-1, 5-1, 5-2
Reviewing word, paragraph, and character counts (e.g., Word Count)	5-5, 5-Lab		
Organize Documents Using File Folders			
Creating and using folders for document storage	1-5		
Renaming folders	8-1		
Saving Documents in Appropriate Formats for Different Uses			
Converting documents to different formats for transportability (e.g., .rtf, .txt)			1-5, 6-1, 1-Lab
Saving documents as Web pages			6-1
Print Documents, Envelopes, and Labels			

Appendix A

Core Skill Sets and Skills Being Measured	Word 2003: Level 1	Word 2003: Level 2	Word 2003: Level 3
Printing documents, envelopes, and labels	1-7	10-3, 10-4	
Preview Documents and Web Pages			
Previewing a document for printing	1-6, 5-6, 1-Lab, 5-Lab	2-Lab	
Previewing a Web page for publication			6-1
Change and Organize Documents Views and Windows			
Revealing formatting and hidden text	3-6		5-3, 5-Lab
Viewing reading layout, normal, outline, full screen, and zoom views	1-6, 5-6, 8-8, 5-Lab		1-3, 2-8
Showing/hiding white space in a document	8-7		
Splitting windows and arrange panes			2-3, 4-6

Expert Skill Sets and Skills Being Measured	Word 2003: Level 1	Word 2003: Level 2	Word 2003: Level 3
Create Custom Styles for Text, Tables, and Lists			
Creating and applying custom styles for text, tables, and lists		4-1, 4-2, 4-3, 4-4, 4-Lab	
Control Pagination			
Controlling orphans and widows		3-3	
Setting line and page breaks	2-3, 8-7, 8-8		
Format, Position, and Resize Graphics Using Advanced Layout Features			
Wrapping text with graphics		5-3, 6-1, 6-3	
Cropping and rotating graphics		5-2	
Controlling image contrast and brightness		5-1	
Scaling and resizing graphics	7-2	5-2	
Insert and Modify Objects			
Inserting and modifying new objects and objects from files			1-1, 1-2, 1-Lab
Create and Modify Diagrams and Charts Using Data From Other Sources			
Creating and revising charts using data from other sources (e.g., Excel)			1-2
Sort Content in Lists and Tables			
Sorting content in lists and tables by specific categories		1-1, 1-2, 2-1, 1-Lab, 2-Lab	

Expert Skill Sets and Skills Being Measured	Word 2003: Level 1	Word 2003: Level 2	Word 2003: Level 3
Perform calculations in tables			
Using formulas in tables		2-6, 2-Lab	
Modify Table Formats			
Modifying table formats by merging and/or splitting table cells		2-3	
Modifying text position and direction in a cell		2-4, 2-Lab	
Modifying table properties		2-4, 4-4	
Inserting and modifying fields		9-7	
Summarize Document Content Using Automated Tools			
Summarize relevant content using automated tools (e.g., AutoSummarize)			4-8
Analyzing content readability using automated tools (e.g., Readability Statistics)	5-2		
Use Automated Tools for Document Navigation			
Inserting Bookmarks			3-1, 3-Lab
Using automation features for document navigation (e.g., Document Map, Thumbnails)			2-8, 3-2, 3-4, 4-2, 4-4
Merge Letters With Other Data Sources			
Completing an entire mail merge process for form letters		10-6, 10-Lab	
Merge Labels With Other Data Sources			
Completing an entire mail merge process for mailing labels		10-2, 10-3, 10-5, 10-6	
Structure Documents Using XML			
Adding, deleting, updating, and modifying schemas, solutions, and settings in the Schema Library			8-1, 8-5, 8-Lab
Adding, deleting, and modifying schemas and transforms to documents			8-1, 8-4, 8-5, 8-Lab
Managing elements and attributes in XML documents (e.g., adding, changing, deleting, cutting, copying)			8-2
Defining XML options (e.g., applying schema validation options, applying XML view options)			8-2, 8-3, 8-Lab
Create and Modify Forms			
Creating and modifying forms			7-1

Expert Skill Sets and Skills Being Measured	Word 2003: Level 1	Word 2003: Level 2	Word 2003: Level 3
Setting and changing options on form fields and check boxes			7-1
Create and Modify Document Background			
Creating watermarks	7-3, 7-Lab		
Applying themes			6-4
Creating and modifying document background colors and fill effects			6-4
Create and Modify Document Indexes and Tables			
Creating and modifying document indexes, tables of content, figures, and authorities			4-2, 4-3, 4-5, 4-6, 4-Lab
Insert and Modify Endnotes, Footnotes, Captions, and Crossreferences			
Inserting format and modifying endnotes, footnotes, captions, and crossreferences			3-2, 3-3, 3-4, 3-Lab
Formatting numbering and marks for footnotes and endnotes			3-2
Create and Manage Master Documents and Subdocuments			
Creating master documents with three or more subdocuments			4-7, 4-Lab
Modify Track Changes Options			
Setting reviewer's ink colors, setting balloon options, showing and hiding reviewers			2-5, 2-8
Publish and Edit Web Documents			
Setting Web options and saving to a Web server			6-1
Inserting and modifying frames			6-5
Manage Document Versions			
Creating, viewing, deleting versions of documents			2-2, 2-Lab
Protect and Restrict Forms and Documents			
Setting formatting restrictions			5-4
Setting editing restrictions			5-5, 7-2, 5-Lab
Adding users excepted from restrictions (groups and individuals)			5-5
Applying passwords to documents and forms			5-7, 7-2, 5-Lab
Attach Digital Signatures to Documents			
Using digital signatures to authenticate documents			5-6
Customize Document Properties			

Expert Skill Sets and Skills Being Measured	Word 2003: Level 1	Word 2003: Level 2	Word 2003: Level 3
Inserting and editing summary and custom information in document properties			2-1, 5-1, 5-2, 5-Lab
Create, Edit, and Run Macros			
Creating and running macros		8-1, 8-2, 8-Lab	
Editing a macro using the Visual Basic Editor		8-3, 8-Lab	
Customize Menus and Toolbars			
Creating a custom menu		8-6	
Adding and removing buttons from a toolbar		8-4, 8-5, 8-Lab	
Modify Word Default Settings			
Changing the default file location for templates		9-5	
Setting default dictionary	5-4		
Modifying default font settings		9-4	

NOTES

LESSON LABS

Due to classroom setup constraints, some labs cannot be keyed in sequence immediately following their associated lesson. Your instructor will tell you whether your labs can be practiced immediately following the lesson or whether they require separate setup from the main lesson content.

LESSON 1 LAB 1

Creating a Document

Activity Time:

10 minutes

Setup:

Word is running with no documents open.

Scenario:

You work in the Human Resources Department and your manager has handed you her notes regarding a new HMO that will soon be available. She has asked you to type it up as an inter-office memo that, when printed, can be distributed to all employees. Figure 1-A shows your manager's notes.

We will soon offer a new HMO plan
from Doctors Unlimited to all employees.
Costs are lower without sacrificing
coverage. More details to come.

Figure 1-A: *Your manager's notes for the new HMO memo.*

Compare your work to Solutions\Benefits Memo Lab Done.doc.

1. In a new document, **enter the memo text.** (See Figure 1-A.)

2. **Save the document as *My Benefits Memo*.**

3. Before you print the memo, to make sure you have all necessary text, **preview the document.**

4. **Print a copy of the memo for your manager then close the document.**

LESSON 2 LAB 1

Editing a Document

Activity Time:

10 minutes

Data Files:

- Facility Request Lab.doc
- Building Security Lab.doc

Setup:

Word is running with no documents open.

Scenario:

Your manager is giving you more responsibility when it comes to editing procedure documents for the Human Resources department. She has a draft document and needs you to edit it.

Compare your work to Solutions\Facility Request Lab Done.doc.

1. **Open Facility Request Lab.**

2. In the first sentence, **"We have created a Facility Request Form," after Facility Request Form, insert the text *(FRF)*.**

3. To the end of the document, **replace any remaining instances of "a Facility Request Form" with the phrase "an FRF".**

4. **Delete the paragraph that begins with "More than any other document...".**

5. **Copy the phone numbers from the end of the Building Security Lab document and paste them at the bottom of the Facility Request Lab document.**

6. **Save the document as *My Facility Request Lab* and then close it.**

LESSON 3 LAB 1

Formatting Text

Data Files:

- Formatting Text Lab.doc

Scenario:

The manager at Books & Beyond is relying on you more and more. As the assistant to the manager, one of your responsibilities is to apply finishing touches to her company correspondence. For your next assignment, you've been given a document that your manager has already typed. You need to apply text formatting to it.

Compare your work to Solutions\Formatting Text Lab Done.doc.

1. **Open the Formatting Text Lab document.**
2. In the first line, **format "Books & Beyond" as Tahoma, 18 pt, bold.**
3. In the next line, **format "Welcome to Our World of Reading and Relaxation" to Tahoma, 14 pt, italic.**
4. **Make the underlined inline headings Tahoma, 11 pt.**
5. **Replace all instances of underline text formatting with bold small caps.**
6. **Highlight the text of your choice and then change the highlight color to a color of your choice.**
7. **Save the document as *My Formatting Text Lab* and close it.**

LESSON 4 LAB 1

Formatting Paragraphs

Data Files:

- Formatting Paragraphs Lab.doc

Scenario:

Since your last assignment went so well, your manager at Books & Beyond is anxious to get you started on your next task. She now needs you to enhance the document by applying paragraph formatting.

Compare your work to Solutions\Formatting Paragraphs Lab Done.doc.

1. **Open the Formatting Paragraphs Lab document.**
2. At the top of the document, **apply the Heading 1 style to "What is Books & Beyond" and center it.**
3. **Apply Heading 2 styles to "Other Special Services" and "How Are We Doing So Far?"**
4. **Change the paragraph headings so that there is a 6-pt space after each paragraph heading.**
5. Under "Other Special Services," **format the paragraphs as a bulleted list.**
6. For the Top Music Categories tabbed text, **change the left indent to 1.75 inches, the right indent to 4.25 inches, and center the heading.**
7. In the tabbed text, **set right tab stops at 3.25 inches and 4.25 inches.**
8. **Apply a box border to the Top Music Categories tabbed text.**
9. **Save the document as *My Formatting Paragraphs Lab* and then close it.**

LESSON 5 LAB 1

Proofing a Document

Data Files:

- Proofing Lab.doc

Scenario:

You have completed a client letter and it's time to proof the document, making corrections as necessary. The word count should be below 200 words. As you preview the document full screen, add the current date and verify that the client's address and closing sections will line up when the letter is printed.

Compare your work to Solutions\Proofing Lab Done.doc.

1. **Open the Proofing Lab document.**
2. **Use the Thesaurus to change some instances of the word "business" with synonyms of your choice.**
3. **Spell check the document, correcting spelling and grammar errors as needed.**
4. **Verify that the letter has 200 words or fewer.**
5. **Preview the letter full screen to verify that the client's address and the closing align properly.**
6. In Print Preview, **add the current date below the client's address.**
7. **Save the letter as *My Proofing Lab* and then close it.**

LESSON 6 LAB 1

Adding Tables

Data Files:

- Table Lab.doc

Scenario:

Your next task is to create formatted tables using a document provided by your co-worker. You have also been asked to add a new table that includes the various types of top selling audio books.

Compare your work to Solutions\Table Lab Done.doc.

1. **Open the Table Lab document.**

2. **Convert the Top Selling Music Categories tabbed text into a table and AutoFormat it using a table format of your choice.**

3. Below the Top Selling Audio Book Categories heading, **create a new table to accommodate the following text:**

Category	Sales
Biography	1,589
Fiction	3,972
Hobby/Recreation	2,975
Youth	756

4. **Apply an AutoFormat to the new table so that its formatting matches the other table.**

5. **Save the document as *My Table Lab* and then close it.**

LESSON 7 LAB 1

Inserting Graphic Elements

Data Files:

- Graphic Elements Lab.doc

Scenario:

You need to complete a one-page flyer promoting the upcoming "Get Published" seminar.

Compare your work to Solutions\Graphic Elements Lab Done.doc.

1. **Open the Graphic Elements Lab document.**
2. **Insert a book-related clip at the top of the document, sizing as needed to keep the flyer to one page.**
3. In the first paragraph of text, **insert the appropriate symbols after the words "copyright" and "trademark."**
4. **Format the background with a watermark that indicates that the seminar is free to the public.**
5. **Save the document as *My Graphic Elements Lab* and then close it.**

LESSON 8 LAB 1

Controlling Page Appearance

Data Files:

- Page Setup Lab.doc

Scenario:

The shop manager made some formatting suggestions for the "Get Published" flyer. You need to implement those suggestions.

Compare your work to Solutions\Page Setup Lab Done.doc.

1. **Open the Page Setup Lab document.**
2. **Make the document landscape.**
3. **Reduce the margins to get the text on a single page.**
4. **Add a box border to the page.**
5. **In the footer, insert the date.**
6. **Save the document as *My Page Setup Lab* and then close it.**

SOLUTIONS

Lesson 1

Activity 1-4

5. **What do you notice about the word "Schyler"?**

   A wavy red underline appears below "Schyler" because the Check Spelling As You Type option is on by default. Word thinks "Schyler" is a misspelled word.

7. **What do you notice about the sentence "(The one on Elm Street.)"?**

   A wavy green underline appears below "(The one on Elm Street.)" because the Check Grammar As You Type option is on by default. Since the sentence does not contain a verb, Word considers it an incomplete sentence.

   As you were typing, the sentence automatically wrapped to the next line.

9. **After typing "teh" and pressing the Spacebar, what was automatically corrected?**

   ✓ a) The word was capitalized.

   b) Nothing.

   c) The word was marked as a grammatical error.

   ✓ d) The misspelling was corrected.

   e) The word was deleted.

Activity 1-5

1. **In the title bar, the file name*Document1* indicates that the document has not been saved yet.**

5. **You can tell that the file has been saved because the new file name is displayed in the*Title bar* .**

Activity 1-6

4. **True or False? In Print Preview, you can see formatting marks, as well as spelling and grammar marks?**

   ___ True

   _✓_ False

Activity 1-7

2. **What print options might you use at your office? Why?**

   Answers will vary, but may include: Select a different printer to print documents in color; select a print range to print only the necessary pages; change the number of copies to print handouts for a meeting; or change the number of pages printed per sheet to conserve paper.

Lesson 2

Activity 2-2

1. **By default, when a document is opened, the insertion point is located at the** *top* **of the document.**

3. **As you scrolled, what information in the status bar changed?**

   The page number information changed.

4. **As you scrolled, did the location of the insertion point change? How can you tell?**

   No, the insertion point did not move. You could tell because the line and column number information did not change in the status bar.

6. **As you used keyboard navigation techniques, did the location of the insertion point change? How can you tell?**

   Yes. As the insertion point moved, changes in vertical position, line number, and column number were reflected in the status bar.

7. **How many pages are in the document?** *3*

Activity 2-4

7. **What happens to text when you select it?**

   Answers will vary, but may include: The text becomes highlighted; the text turns white with a black background; the text is shaded.

8. **Do you find selecting text easier using the mouse, the keyboard, or a combination of both?**

   Answers will vary, but may include: It's easier to select text with the mouse because you can make small or large selections with little difficulty. It's easier to select text with the keyboard because it's easier to control the selection. It's easier to combine both methods because you can quickly place the insertion point (mouse) and use Shift to extend the selection.

Activity 2-5

4. How might you use AutoText on your job?

   Answers will vary, but may include: To quickly insert a typical legal disclaimer paragraph; to add a closing to a form letter; to insert directions to an office location; and so on.

Activity 2-8

2. Is the deleted text added to the Clipboard task pane? *No.*

4. After deleting the text block, can you paste it somewhere else? *No.*

Lesson 3

Activity 3-6

2. In the Reveal Formatting task pane's Formatting Of Selected Text list box, the font attributes include: (Default) Times New Roman, 12 pt, and *Italic* .

3. The only Character Options listed in the Formatting Of Selected Text list box is *Highlight* .

5. Using the Reveal Formatting task pane, which Font attribute was cleared? *Italic*

6. True or False? The highlighting was cleared, too.

   __ True

   ✓ False

Lesson 4

Activity 4-4

5. The disclaimer text's top and bottom borders extend to the Left and Right *indent markers* , not the left and right margins.

Lesson 5

Activity 5-3

4. What is the percentage of passive sentences in the document?*4%*

Activity 5-4

2. What is the name of the current default dictionary?*Custom.dic*

7. True or False? "Beantown," "BurkeBuddy," and "TeamServe" are listed in the Product Names.dic.

   ✓ True

   __ False

Activity 5-5

3. How many words are in the selection?*19*

5. How many words are in the document after the deletion?*272*

Activity 5-6

5. What's the font size of all the text in the document?*11*

6. Why isn't the text 12 pt?

   Because the Shrink To Fit command reduces the font size for all text in a document to reduce page count. To fit this document on one page, it only had to reduce the font size to 11 pt.

Lesson 6

Activity 6-1

1. Based upon the text provided by your manager, how many rows will you include in the table?*5*

2. Based upon the text provided by your manager, how many columns will you include in the table?*4*

4. **Where is the insertion point?**

   a) Before the table.

   b) After the table.

   ✓ c) In the first cell of the table.

   d) In the last cell of the table.

   e) At the top of the document.

5. **Which non-printing characters are displayed in the table?**

   ✓ a) End-of-row markers.

   ✓ b) End-of-cell markers.

   c) End-of-column markers.

   d) End-of-table markers.

Activity 6-5

1. **Using text formatting techniques, how might you make the table text more readable?**

   Bold the column heading text.

   Italicize the March totals.

   Bold the text in the Total row.

4. **What kind of formatting do you notice being applied to the text and table in the Preview area?**

   Font style changes (bold and italic).

   Table borders change thickness and color.

   Columns and rows are shaded with different colors.

Lesson 7

Activity 7-3

2. **How might you want to change the text watermark?**

   Change the font.

   Change the font size.

   Change the color.

   Change the layout.

3. **How might you use watermarks in your documents?**

   To show document status (FIRST DRAFT, FINAL, and so on).

   To show corporate or product branding (MY COMPANY NAME or logo, XYZ Product Name, and so on).

   To show instructions (DO NOT COPY, DO NOT DISTRIBUTE, and so on).

Lesson 8

Activity 8-7

1. **How many pages are in the document currently?***2*

Activity 8-8

2. **How many pages is the document now?***2*

GLOSSARY

border
A decorative line or pattern that is displayed around an object, such as a paragraph, picture, or page.

custom dictionary
A list of words and terms that will be ignored by Word's spell-checking features.

expanded menu
A menu that displays all available options.

field
A set of instructions that acts as a placeholder in a document. Each field is used to display specific pieces of information, such as the current date or time.

font
A named set of characters that combines several design qualities, such as a typeface and font style.

footer
The blank area in a page's bottom margin. Ordinarily repeated throughout a document, a footer can contain textual or graphical information to provide context for the reader.

Format Painter
A tool on the Standard toolbar used to copy character or paragraph formatting from one selection to another.

formatting mark
A non-printing character, such as a space, paragraph, or tab, that is displayed in the text area. The mark acts as a placeholder and identifies when a formatting key has been pressed.

header
The blank area in a page's top margin. Ordinarily repeated throughout a document, a header can contain textual or graphical information to provide context for the reader.

indent
A way to align a paragraph's left and right edges without changing the margins for the entire document.

landscape
A page positioned horizontally so that it is wider than it is tall.

line break
A formatting mark used to end the current line manually before it wraps to the next line automatically.

list
A way to present information separately from the surrounding text.

main dictionary
The primary dictionary used to check a document's spelling. The main dictionary is neither editable nor viewable.

margin
The area of white space along the top, bottom, left, and right edges of a page. Margins determine the size of the document's text area.

portrait
A page positioned vertically so that it is taller than it is wide.

readability statistics
Detailed information about a document, including counts, averages, and readability scores.

ScreenTip
A descriptive label that is displayed when you position the mouse pointer over various items in the program window, such as a toolbar button.

selection handles
Small black squares that appear around a selected clip. Selection handles can be dragged to resize the clip.

shading
A percentage of color that can be added to the background of an object, like text, paragraph, or table data.

short menu
A menu that displays only the most commonly used options.

special characters
Uncommon punctuation, spacing, and typographical characters that are not readily available on the standard keyboard.

style
A set of formatting instructions that is stored under one name. When the style is applied, all of the formatting instructions are applied to text simultaneously and consistently.

symbol
Text characters that are not readily available on the standard keyboard.

tab stop
A mark on the horizontal ruler that indicates where and what type of tab is set in the paragraph where the insertion point is located. A tab stop enables you to line up text to the left, right, center, or to a decimal character or bar character. Also referred to generically as a tab.

Thesaurus
A reference book available in the Research task pane that can be used to look up potential synonyms—words with similar meanings—and antonyms—words with opposite meanings.

watermark
A graphical element that, when printed, appears behind a document's text.

INDEX